THE
JAPANESE
HOUSE
REINVENTED

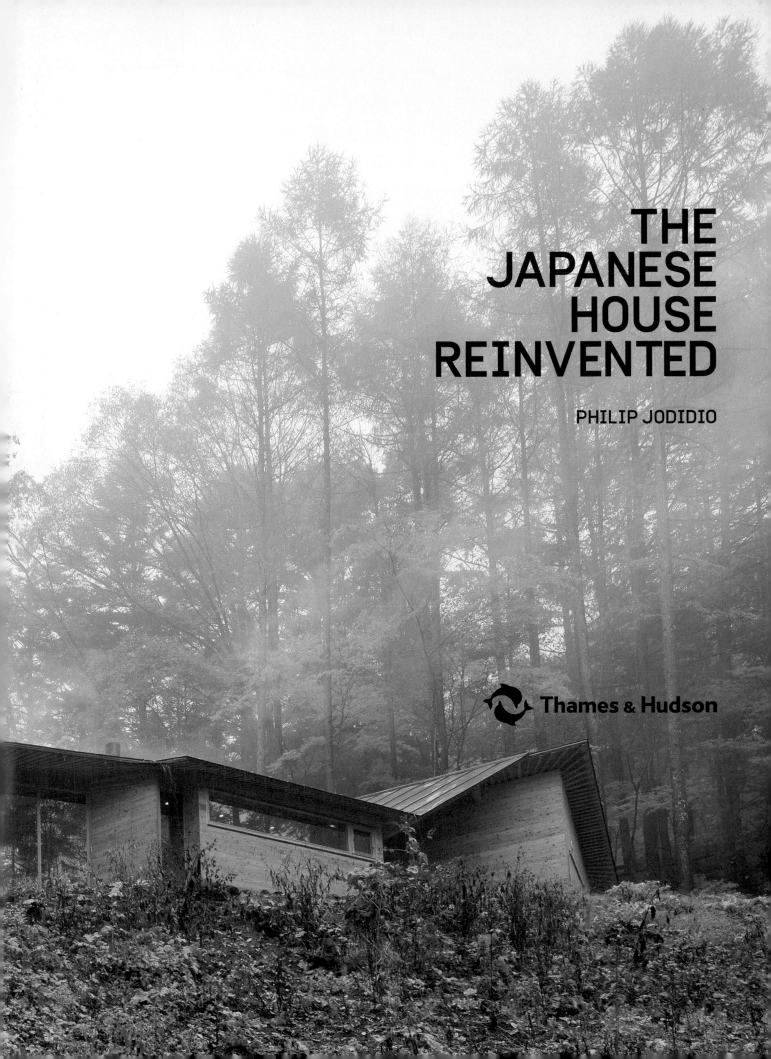

THE
JAPANESE
HOUSE
REINVENTED

PHILIP JODIDIO

Thames & Hudson

First published in the United Kingdom in 2015 by
Thames & Hudson Ltd, 181A High Holborn,
London WC1V 7QX

British Library Cataloguing-in-Publication Data
A catalogue record for this book is available from the
British Library

ISBN 978-0-500-34308-1

Printed and bound in China

To find out about all our publications, please visit
www.thamesandhudson.com.
There you can subscribe to our e-newsletter, browse or
download our current catalogue, and buy any titles
that are in print.

Contents

INTRODUCTION

Houses at the Edge

Japan, like the United States, has long shown a preference for houses as opposed to apartments. Recent surveys indicate that about 60% of Japanese dwellings are single-family homes. Those who have travelled in Japan, notably on such rapid train lines as the Shinkansen that links Tokyo to Osaka, can comprehend the sheer quantity of such structures, often marked by a vaguely understood "Oriental" feature, such as a tiled roof. Clearly, the majority of these houses are of a repetitive or architecturally uninteresting nature, but by way of contrast, there are also a high number of inventive contemporary houses in the country, some of which are the subject of this publication. Faced with the constraints of very dense urban areas and a lifestyle that has long taken into account small spaces, Japanese architects and their clients have shown a surprising willingness to experiment.

While Western eyes see little presence of nature in Japanese cities, the Japanese themselves perceive views of the sky or sunlight inside a house as manifestations of nature, an important element in day-to-day existence. A clear trend has emerged in recent years to open interior spaces of Japanese houses, much as sliding *shoji* screens allowed a high degree of flexibility in the past. Intermediate floor levels and spaces that are surprisingly open characterize many contemporary houses, with privacy expressed in more succinct terms than in many Western homes. This openness obviously is one way of addressing the small spaces that even relatively wealthy Japanese must make do with, especially in cities such as Tokyo and Osaka. What makes Japanese houses original and interesting is surely a matter of culture and lifestyle, but is also driven by a large number of persons who are ready to take risks, either in designing these houses, or in living in them. Some may feel that a culture is expressed in superficial details like

In the urban areas of Japan, nature is strictly limited to existing parks or small green areas. The density of construction does not allow for a great deal of planting. For this reason, interior courtyards or planted passageways such as these are quite popular. Even the limited presence of plants, daylight, and a hint of breeze are taken as expressions of nature that are a relief from the congestion of the city.

tiled, upturned roofs, but in the houses published here, the "Japanese" nature of the architecture is most deeply expressed in the perception of space and nature.

Slightly smaller than California, Japan has more than three times its population, estimated at just over 127 million in 2014. Certainly the largest urban concentration in the world, Tokyo is home to more than 37 million persons compressed into 0.6% of the total area of Japan, creating an extreme density of more than 36,260 persons per square mile in the city's central wards. A large part of the eastern seaboard of the country, spanning 310 miles between Tokyo and Osaka, is almost a continuous urban area, while to the west there are more mountainous and less densely settled areas. These facts, and in particular the urban density of the country (91.3% of total population lived in urban areas in 2011), are important in understanding its architecture, particularly where residential construction is concerned. The Japanese are accustomed to conditions of crowding, and as can readily be seen in this book, sites offered for construction are often very small by Western standards, with the obvious corollary being that Japanese homes are usually diminutive by comparison.

Although its population has been slowing increasing, Japan rates 222nd in the world in terms of its birth rate (8.07 births/1,000 population in 2014 estimates). The essential fact about Japanese demography is that its population is aging.

Twice Destroyed, Ever Rebuilt

Another significant factor in Japanese architecture is the underlying sense of fragility born of catastrophes. Successive disasters, some natural and some man-made, have shaped the contemporary face of major Japanese cities. The first of these in the twentieth century was the Great Kanto Earthquake of 1923. Measuring 7.9 on the Richter scale, the quake and subsequent fires and tsunami killed around 200,000 people primarily in Tokyo and Yokohama, leaving 64% of the remaining population homeless. The second catastrophe, even more radical in its destruction, was the firebombing of Tokyo between March and May of 1945. More people died in these months than in the instantaneous devastations of Hiroshima and Nagasaki. By September 1945, the population of the city, which exceeded 6.9 million in 1942, plunged through death and emigration to 2.77 million. Incendiary devices, dropped on a city constituted mostly of wooden structures at the time, were particularly devastating. For this reason, it can be said that the most populous city on earth has been rebuilt almost entirely since 1945. At the outset, this construction went forward with limited means. As in war-torn Europe, it was essential to build cheaply and fast. In more recent times, implacable commercial logic has trumped the canons of tradition or esthetics. In a sense, an explosion of bad architecture is the second man-made disaster that has marked Tokyo's recent history. It has swept before it much of the beauty of centuries-old tradition.

Heavy and Light

In general, contemporary Japanese architects have reacted in two distinct ways to the peculiarities of their environment—in philosophical terms and in their choice of building materials. They arguably start from a position of reaction—a response to an earth likely to tremble at any moment, producing the need to make buildings as stable as possible. Particularly since 1981, strict laws have governed the solidity of buildings and public works. This fact, together with an allied aesthetic approach, can often explain why certain modern structures in Japan seem to be unusually massive, sitting on the earth as though waiting to pit their strength against natural upheavals. Numerous Japanese architects are clearly devoted to the double role that concrete plays, providing both strong structure and sculptural possibility. Elevated roadways, bridges, or the steel skeletons of new buildings have an obligatory density here that tends to define their final appearance more so than in other countries. Houses too often display a considerable amount of reinforced concrete. A second, almost contradictory, direction in contemporary architecture tends toward an airy lightness that may trace its origin back to traditional wooden buildings. Like ships, these structures seem to hope to ride out the impending storm by floating on the land or even in the air. Houses made of light steel and large windows are just as plentiful as the heavier concrete sort. Just as a love for kitsch and a profound respect for the subtle beauties of tradition exist side by side in Japan, so does the dichotomy of weight and lightness inform its architecture.

Sunshine Rights

Though war has not been an obvious concern for Japan in the early twenty-first century, cataclysmic earthquakes—such as those that devastated Kobe on January 17, 1995, or the more recent Tōhoku earthquake and tsunami of March 11, 2011—are still very much part of the Japanese psyche. The eventuality of a severe earthquake in Tokyo is by no means ignored, rather it is the subject of constant preparation and public debate. Particularly for the Western visitor, Tokyo at first glance is an almost infinite jumble of coiled and dangling electrical wires and small, unsightly buildings. Aside from esthetic considerations, there are two good reasons for the unusual

appearance of much of Tokyo, and indeed of most other Japanese cities. One is that it is forbidden for any two buildings to share a structural wall. A tiny passageway between walls naturally limits the danger that the collapse of one building during an earthquake will cause a chain reaction. The second is the so-called *nisshoken,* or sunshine rights, that theoretically require that any new building not deprive its neighbors of more than a certain amount of natural light. Although sunshine rights are variously applied and rarely the object of legal action, this laudable measure has resulted in the odd positions of many structures in their lots. Though apartment buildings have been built to the horizon and beyond in Tokyo and elsewhere, there is still a culture of the private house in Japan, and these houses for the reasons described never touch each other, even when they form rows. Even in small lots they also tend to be idiosyncratically oriented for reasons of privacy, light, or more prosaically to create a space to park the owner's car.

Breaking Free

The emergence of modern Japanese architecture can be viewed in terms of a progressive liberation from Western influences. When Commodore Perry viewed the city of Edo during his 1853—54 expedition, he described it as an "extensive plain with a magnificent background of mountains and wooded country." The far-reaching consequences of the Perry Expedition have been extensively analyzed, but it should be recalled that as early as 1872 the Meiji government called on the British architect and planner Thomas Waters to rebuild the sector to the southeast of the Imperial Palace, destroyed in that year by a fire. Waters laid out neoclassical buildings along a broad avenue that came to be known as the Ginza. Another Englishman, Josiah Conder (1852—1920), built numerous heavy Second Empire style masonry buildings, such as the National Museum in Ueno Park (1882), that became the symbols of the Japanese establishment until the Ministry of the Cabinet decided to call on the Germans Hermann Ende (1829—1907) and Wilhelm Böckmann (1832—1902). Their plan for a Prussian-style building for the Japanese Diet, capped with a pagoda-like form, met with concerted opposition and calls for a resolution between indigenous and Western architectural styles.

"There was sixty to seventy feet of soft mud below the upper depth of eight feet of surface soil on the site. That mud seemed a merciful provision—a good cushion to relieve the terrible shocks. Why not float the building upon it? A battleship floats on salt water." This is how another foreign architect in Japan, Frank Lloyd Wright, described his plans for the Imperial Hotel in Tokyo (1916—22). Demolished amid controversy in 1967 to make way for a more modern structure, this eccentric structure famously survived the devastating earthquake of

Often faced with the challenge of making the most of small spaces in houses, Japanese architects have proven to be particularly inventive in the design of stairways. A moveable wooden staircase might double as a bookshelf or storage space, for instance (bottom right). Other stairs can become a study in the minimal expression of function.

1923, adding to Wright's reputation, not least of all in Japan. Wright was of course not the only Western architect to have exerted an influence on the development of modern Japanese architecture. Le Corbusier, for example, who continues to fascinate many contemporary architects, made his presence felt through projects such as the National Museum of Western Art in Ueno Park in Tokyo (1959) and through the work of early native modernists such as Kunio Maekawa, who worked in Le Corbusier's atelier in France from 1928 to 1930 before establishing his own office in Tokyo in 1935. Maekawa completed the 1979 addition to the National Museum of Western Art, symbolically reaffirming the importance of Le Corbusier in Japan.

Discovering Katsura

On November 4, 1935, the German architect Bruno Taut (1880–1938) wrote in his journal, "I can truly claim to be the discoverer of Katsura." This affirmation, concerning the seventeenth-century imperial residence located near Kyoto, is of considerable importance for the evolution of contemporary Japanese architecture. While the Japanese had in various ways absorbed the Western influences to which they were subjected after the Perry Expedition, they had come to reject many aspects of their own tradition. Thus the rise of fascism in Japan was accompanied by a certain rejection of Western-inspired modernity in favor of an architecture called *teikan yoshiki* or the "Imperial roof style," which featured heavy cubic structures capped by equally ungainly "Japanese" roofs. Having arrived in Japan in May 1933, Taut spent three and a half years writing about Katsura, linking its elegant simplicity to the goals of the modern movement and calling it an "eternal monument." As Arata Isozaki points out, other Western architects, such as the German Gustav Prattz, had visited Katsura even before Taut, and had integrated its lessons into "the renewal of world architecture." The rediscovery of the fundamental links between Japanese tradition and modernism itself occurred only after the trauma of World War II, partly because the very idea of calling on tradition had been misappropriated by a largely discredited political ideology.

From Kenzo Tange to Shigeru Ban

The post-War rediscovery of Japanese tradition by the Japanese themselves was aided by figures such as the architect Kenzo Tange. Born in 1913, Tange had worked in the 1930s in the office of Kunio Maekawa, but his Olympic Sports Halls for the 1964 Tokyo Olympics announced the emergence of an essentially indigenous modernity on a par in terms of quality and inventiveness with that of the West. Author of the Hiroshima Peace Park and Museum, a moving testimony to the terrifying impact of the atomic bomb, Tange, who died in 2005, remains a symbol of modern Japanese architecture. However, his late work, such as the Tokyo City Hall, an 800-foot-tall double tower that occupies three full blocks in the Shinjuku area (1991), is considered by many to be a symbol of the excesses of the Bubble years of the late 1980s and early 90s.

If international awards such as the Pritzker Prize are any indication, contemporary Japanese architecture has emerged as a substantial force on the international scene in recent years, beginning with Tange himself, who won the coveted Prize in 1987. Since then, Japanese winners of the Pritzker are Fumihiko Maki (1993), Tadao Ando (1995), Kazuyo Sejima and Ryue Nishizawa SANAA (2010), Toyo Ito (2013), and Shigeru Ban (2014). Though each of these architects has worked with Japanese tradition in different ways, sometimes even denying its significance, it seems clear that the very particular conditions of contemporary Japanese architecture have been nourished by a rich tradition that has been found to have many similarities with the "simplicity" of modern architecture in general. It is a testimony to the importance of residential architecture in Japan that such Pritzker-winners as Tadao Ando (House in Utsubo Park, Osaka, 2010, page 30), Shigeru Ban (Villa in Sengokuhara, Hakone, Kanagawa, 2013, page 66; Yakushima Takatsuka Lodge, Yakushima, Kagoshima, 2013, page 72), and Kazuyo Sejima (Tsuchihashi House, Tokyo, 2012, page 240) are still actively building houses.

A Ray of Sunlight

The architecture of contemporary Japanese houses is the result of a number of influences that are largely absent from their Western equivalents. The issue of impermanence, as manifested in the constant risk of earthquake, informs many of the designs seen in this book, but so too does tradition. Thus such frequently evoked concepts as that of *engawa* (veranda) find numerous manifestations in the architects' desire to develop an ambiguous relationship between interior and exterior, and finally perhaps between natural and man-made. Even such a basic concept as the definition of nature differs between Japan and most Western countries. Where an American might think of vast empty spaces or majestic mountain ranges when nature is evoked, a Japanese person can conceive of a ray of sunlight and the feeling of the breeze as being manifestations of nature that are an essential part of the houses published here. It will strike some that many of these houses look particularly "closed" from the outside, yet inside natural light and even outdoor space are almost always part of the concept.

Inner Freedom

Small residential spaces that developed over time due to conditions of crowding and the cost of land are nearly omnipresent in Japanese residential architecture. Some exceptions of course occur, but mainly outside of the major cities. Crowding may also at least partially explain another form of ambiguity present in Japanese houses. While architects carefully design walls and other barriers to preserve the privacy of their clients, it seems that the interiors of these houses are frequently very open and empty by Western standards. Where closed rooms with specific functions may still be much more frequent in the West, Japan has long mastered the art of the sliding rice paper screen (*shoji*) that both filters light and allows interior spaces to be redefined as required. Surely pressed by extreme conditions of density and limited size, many talented Japanese architects have come to view the task of designing a house as being one that obliges them to look back to the origins of architecture and forward to its future. Houses filled with numerous tiny spaces, or floor levels that are varied with a disconcerting freedom, spaces that intentionally have no specific function: these are all devices used by architects to create what can be seen as a fundamentally free interior space, contrasting with the powerful constraints of space imposed by Japanese cities, but also perhaps the very systems of the society that make each person respect forms of order.

Philip Jodidio
April 2014

Although every type of configuration can be found in Japanese houses, there may be a preference for an indirect approach, a door that does not look like one, or which is placed behind a protecting wall. Entryways are also often characterized by asymmetry, placed to one side for example. An element of surprise makes the visitor notice the entrance and the change of architectural environment that it implies.

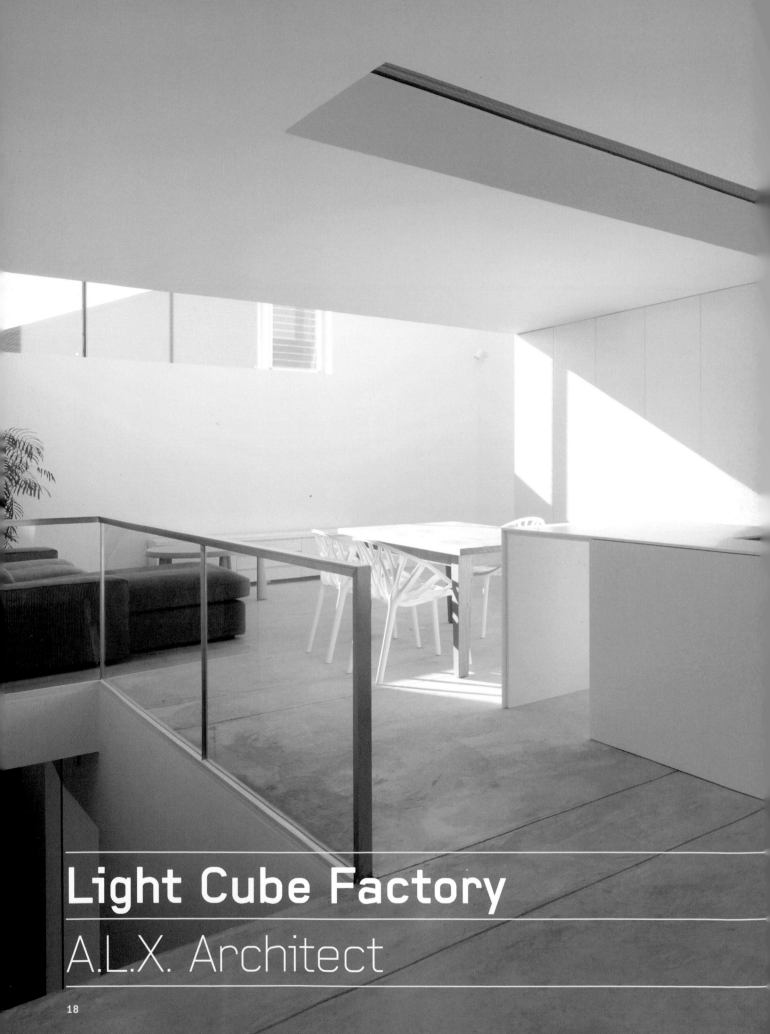

Light Cube Factory
A.L.X. Architect

LOCATION   Tokyo

COMPLETED   2011

FLOOR AREA   1,720 ft²

SITE AREA   480 ft²

The strict glass and concrete
composition offers two surprising
features that can be seen from
the house's exterior: the protruding
box on the upper level, and of course
the double-height glazing that opens
directly onto the street.

The house is set in a residential area in which, as is
common in Tokyo, there are few overt alignments, and
houses are frequently set at slightly different angles
to each other. This three-story reinforced concrete
structure contains a studio and residence. The basic
plan is trapezoidal, aligned only partially along the site
boundaries. Despite essentially rectilinear alignments,
spatial surprises are present throughout the design.
Double-height spaces are arranged at the lower front
and upper rear of the house. Sampei designed the ground
floor to be "open to the city," with double-height
glazing permitting a good part of the interior to be
visible from the street. The living room is located on the
second floor, as well as a kitchen island shaped like
the building itself. A rectangular glass box penetrates
from the top-level skylight, through the upper floor,
and is enclosed by a glass ceiling above the kitchen,
admitting natural overhead light.

The architect explains that the flat skylights are
intentional, allowing rain to pool and ripple, animating
the interior light of the house during the day. Next to the
kitchen, a glass cube is cantilevered from the building,
with a small terrace on its roof that is accessible from
the top floor. The master bedroom and a nursery space
are located on the top floor. As is frequently the case
in Japanese architecture, Sampei has sought to render
the relationship between interior and exterior ambiguous.
Above all, the interior design of the house seems to
always be filled with light, opening from one level to the
next in unexpected ways.

Thanks to its skylights and a glass volume positioned both inside and out, the apparently cold design of the house is animated by the constant movement of natural light, augmented on occasion by pooling water on the flat skylights.

A dining table positioned near the street side window seems to voluntarily offer up the owners' privacy to passersby, allowing them to glimpse the minimal design alternating severe opacity with surprising transparency.

White interior volumes interpenetrate each other, inviting in not only light, but the presence of the city itself.

A.L.X. Architect
Junichi Sampei was born in Chiba Prefecture in 1968. He worked in the office of noted architect Shin Takamatsu in Kyoto from 1996 to 1998, before founding A.L.X. in Toyko in 1999.

www.xain.jp/works.html

A   Living/Dining Room
B   Master Bedroom
C   Nursery
D   Terrace
E   Kitchen
F   Storage
G   Entrance
H   Studio

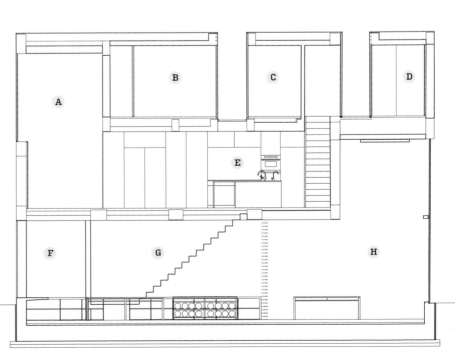

Tokyo House

A.L.X. Architect

LOCATION **Tokyo**

COMPLETED **2010**

FLOOR AREA **840 ft²**

SITE AREA **480 ft²**

The Tokyo House is a three-story reinforced concrete residence with a total floor area just under 850 square feet. A determining condition of this house is its very limited site area, which the architect intentionally stretched to the absolute maximum allowed by city regulations. As a result, the perforated steel-covered structure seems to extend right up to the curbside, not even allowing space for a sidewalk. In its neighborhood, however, this is permitted; nearby houses approach the street in a similar way.

In daylight, the abstract, angled form also has no apparent apertures aside from the entrance door. From within however, the trapezoidal windows are apparent, as is an intriguing use of space, with full-height openings belying the small footprint and floor area of the house. A glass bridge and suspended white metal stairways allow access to the upper areas. Cast-in-place concrete and metal are the main interior materials.

The architect speaks of the "openness to the outside from the inside" in this project that indeed permits ample natural interior light despite an apparently insular appearance. At night, the windows of the building become apparent as they glow from within.

The perforated steel skin of the house suggests openings but does not reveal them. Within, skylights bring light and a view of the sky into the heart of the structure.

A willful play on light is
orchestrated in the interior spaces
where only gray and white surfaces
are allowed. Open stairways and
a glass bridge connect the different
levels.

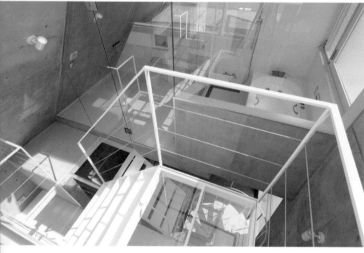

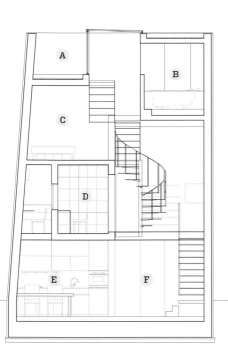

A   Roof Terrace
B   Bathroom
C   Bedroom
D   Study
E   Kitchen/Dining Room
F   Living Room

House in Utsubo Park
Tadao Ando Architect & Assoc.

LOCATION   Osaka

COMPLETED   2010

FLOOR AREA 2,000 ft²

SITE AREA   1,540 ft²

Tadao Ando alternates his trademark
concrete walls with wood surfaces
inside, featuring furniture designed
by the architect himself.

Utsubo Park is one of the few relatively large green
spaces in central Osaka, created on the site of a former
U.S. airfield. This house by Tadao Ando, built to a
fairly generous size in this very dense city, faces the
park on its southern side. Intended for a couple with
two dogs, House in Utsubo Park occupies a narrow but
deep site, enclosed on two sides by mid-rise buildings.
The architect sought to "capture" the green space to
the south, opening a courtyard in that direction. A wall
closes the courtyard at the limit of the site, but is
covered with plants, echoing the nearby park. A double-
height living room, a frequent feature of Ando's houses,
is also set on the house's southern side.

Very simple furnishings and white
pottery alternate with steel-framed
windows, which in the case of the
main space (right) can be entirely
opened.

The north gate opens onto an entrance court, above
which the study cantilevers at the upper level. Ando
has employed the same stone inside and in the courtyards
of the house, emphasizing continuity between interior
and exterior. The private areas of the house are at the
top level with a 30-square-foot roof terrace on the
southern side. Light and wind, elements that typically
symbolize the presence of nature in Japan, pass through
the house; in this instance, greenery is also part of an
equation that makes "the whole building work as a device
that systematically draws 'nature' inside."

Plans show the long, thin form of the
residence, the design appearing
to close out the urban environment
and leave only views of the sky
and greenery.

THIRD FLOOR

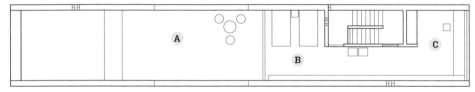

SECOND FLOOR

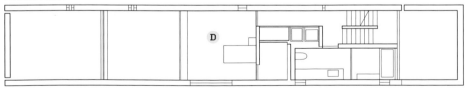

A	Terrace
B	Master Bedroom
C	Study
D	Bedroom
E	Living Room
F	Kitchen/
	Dining Room
G	Entrance
H	Entrance Court

FIRST FLOOR

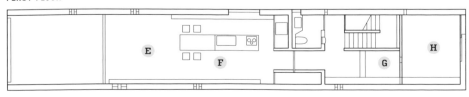

TADAO ANDO ARCHITECT & ASSOC.

Tadao Ando

Tadao Ando (b. 1941) established his design studio, Tadao Ando Architect & Associates, in Osaka in 1968. His designs have won numerous prize, including the Pritzker Architecture Prize in 1995.

tadao-ando.com

HOUSE IN UTSUBO PARK   35

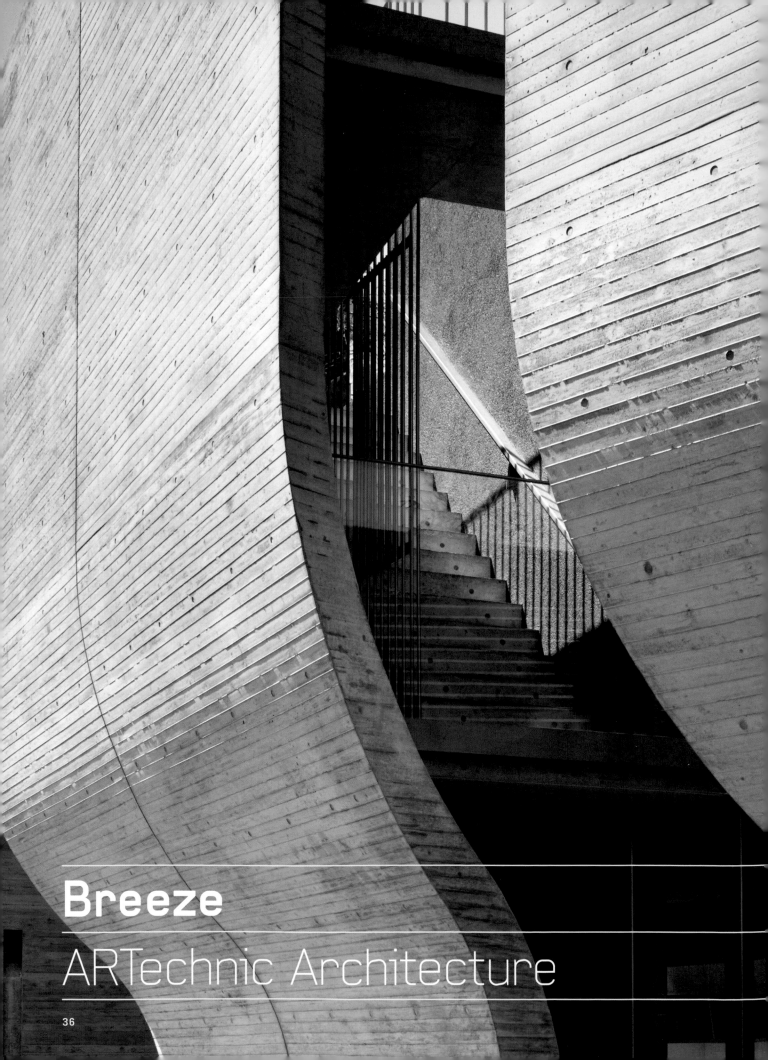

Breeze
ARTechnic Architecture

LOCATION   Tokyo

COMPLETED   2012

FLOOR AREA   13,475 ft²

SITE AREA   5,605 ft²

ARTECHNIC ARCHITECTURE

Three stories high, this residential building soars to
nearly 33 feet above street level. The exterior walls are
concrete covered with polystyrene heat insulating board.
This system was chosen by the architect with the very
clear intention of allowing the building to be resurfaced
easily, as required over time. Inside, the concrete is
painted and walnut plywood impregnated with a urethane
paint finish is used on the walls. The floors are walnut
and concrete with an exposed aggregate finish. A radiant
heating and cooling system through the floors was chosen
for maximum energy efficiency. The architect says
that he "needed to create an exterior that was distinct
from the standard architectural lexicon." He compares
the exterior walls to "a soaring rock face" and the
interior to a "private beach"—a "bolt-hole for personal
rest and relaxation." Located in the Setagaya area
of Tokyo, the house is however very much in the middle of
the largest city on earth.

Architect Kotaro Ide explains, "I decided on
the current layout after considering the most efficient
configuration for each residential unit based on the
building plot, which is long from east to west, short
from south to north, and faces road on the north side.
My idea was that a terrace house style would be the most
efficient given the specifications of the building plot.
I sought to concentrate on bringing out the commercial
appeal of the luxury of space."

The device of the concrete shell,
which could give the house an
oppressive opacity when viewed
from the outside, is rendered more
permeable by the large slit
opening and more inviting by the
upward curve of the façade.

A carefully balanced composition
of wooden floors, a "floating"
stairway, and full-height glazing
makes the interior more inviting
than the exterior might imply.
A sloping green lawn invites nature
into the balance of elements.

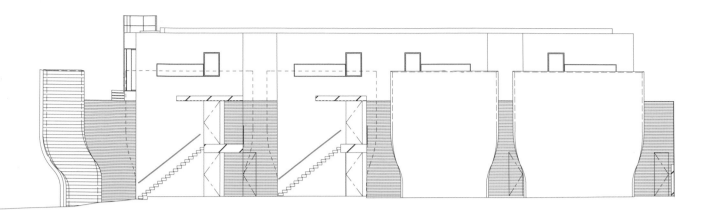

NORTH ELEVATION

ARTechnic Architecture
Kotaro Ide was born in Tokyo in 1965. He worked in the office of Ken Yokogawa Architects from 1989 to 1994, when he established his own office.
www.artechnic.jp

YNO
ARTechnic Architecture

LOCATION   Tokyo

COMPLETED   2012

FLOOR AREA   1,045 ft²

SITE AREA   880 ft²

In detailing the primary design decisions, architect Kotaro Ide explains, "Considering the surrounding environment, I wanted the house to open up, while at the same time maintaining its privacy." Formed by a series of rectangles, both in plan and in section, the house is bordered by parallel metal-mesh screens located four feet from either side of the "bridge-like living room." These screens ensure the privacy of residents and form a "slit space" filled with natural light that leads to the upper level entrance to the house. A frequent feature of Japanese houses, this slit becomes an area that is neither fully outside nor inside the house—it is a transitional space that impedes residents or visitors from penetrating directly into the private interior from the street. The screen reaches up to the handrail of the terrace on the top floor and "works as a reflection panel for the sunlight, increasing the amount of light that reaches the inside of the house." With its horizontal slat facade alternating with concrete surfaces, the house appears to be quite closed from the outside for reasons of privacy, while the interior instead gives an impression of openness. The architect has frequently experimented with simple forms that assume a surprising physical presence. This was notably the case in his dramatic yet modest Shell House (Karuizawa, Nagano, 2008), which as its name implies, essentially forms a reinforced concrete tube or shell.

The house is strict in terms of both its exterior form and its broad flat interior surfaces. Floor plans confirm the grid arrangement of the rectangular design, with stairways placed at the outer edges.

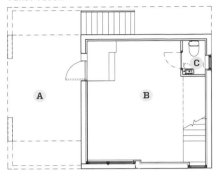

A   B

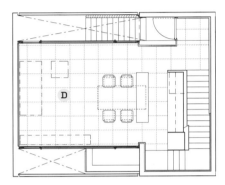

D

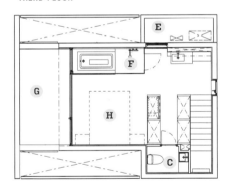

E

F

G   H

C

A	Car Port
B	Study and Storage
C	Lavatory
D	Kitchen/Living Room/
	Dining Room
E	Mechanical Space
F	Bathroom
G	Terrace
H	Bedroom

Double Gable House

Atelier Bow-Wow

LOCATION Kamakura, Kanagawa

COMPLETED 2012

FLOOR AREA 980 ft²

SITE AREA 1,075 ft²

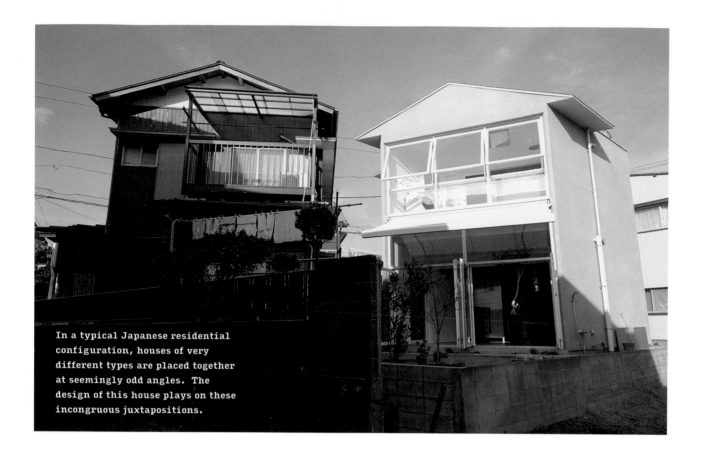

In a typical Japanese residential configuration, houses of very different types are placed together at seemingly odd angles. The design of this house plays on these incongruous juxtapositions.

What at first appears to be a relatively simple or even modest house proves to have a great number of architectural innovations and variations resulting from its irregular plan, which make this space come to life. The exterior walls of this wood-structured house are covered in sand-textured mortar, with an interior surfaced in tropical plywood. The lower level includes a living room/dining room/kitchen space (a common hybrid space in Japan, abbreviated as LDK) and the parents' bedroom and bathroom, while the upper floor includes a music room, a high, narrow children's room, and a terrace. The ground floor "sun room" has full-height glazing with large glass doors that open out onto a garden.

This part of the city exhibits the pervasive irregular street pattern and patchwork assembly of relative small houses, often set at unexpected angles. Almost as an echo to this pattern, the Double Gable House has an irregular plan that takes advantage of the form of the lot. This angled form is echoed closely in such spaces as the music room. Two differently sized gables mark the roof, parting at the uppermost level to leave the open, flat space of the outdoor terrace.

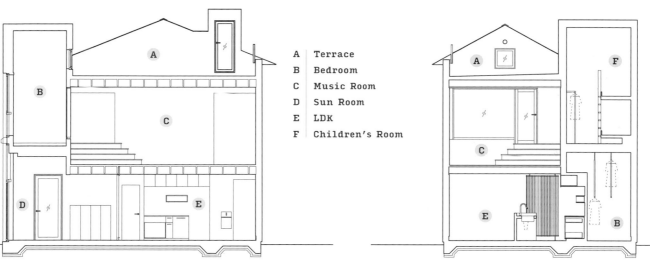

A	Terrace
B	Bedroom
C	Music Room
D	Sun Room
E	LDK
F	Children's Room

DOUBLE GABLE HOUSE

Terrace House

Atelier Bow-Wow

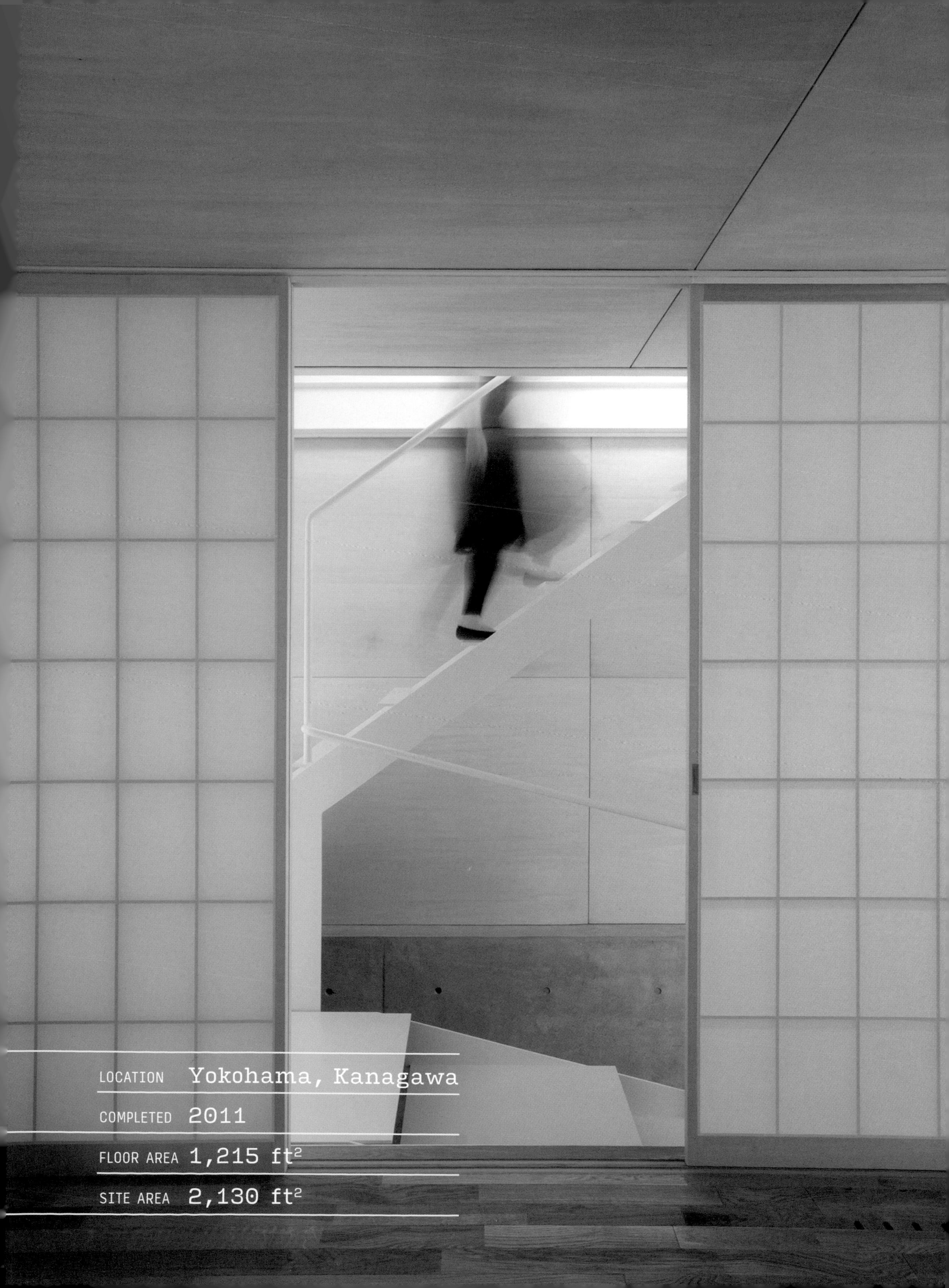

LOCATION   Yokohama, Kanagawa

COMPLETED   2011

FLOOR AREA 1,215 ft²

SITE AREA   2,130 ft²

Set into a rather typical residential street, the Terrace House stands out from its neighbors because it is entirely white and has a stepped-back form, creating terraces and large, recessed glazed openings. With a footprint of just 635 square feet, this rectangular-plan house was built with a steel frame and reinforced concrete. Its exterior walls are finished in plaster, and it has a storage area below grade with exposed concrete walls. A small entrance area with a mosaic tile floor is coupled with a studio space at the lowest ground level. A bedroom and "housework room" a half-level up have solid oak flooring and are faced in Shina, a fairly blemish-free, fine-grained plywood from Hokkaido, notably used in printmaking.

The architects contrast and juxtapose the Shina surfaces with a light steel frame and lower walls in cast-in-place concrete. A steel stairway ascends to a living and dining area opening to the west terrace of the stepped house. On the same level near the east terrace is the kitchen. With its half-levels and *shoji*-like screens, the house combines a certain vision of Japanese tradition with a modernity that redefines space without recourse to "normal" floor levels.

In the midst of a typical clutter of different architectural styles, the Terrace House stands out and imposes its calm order.

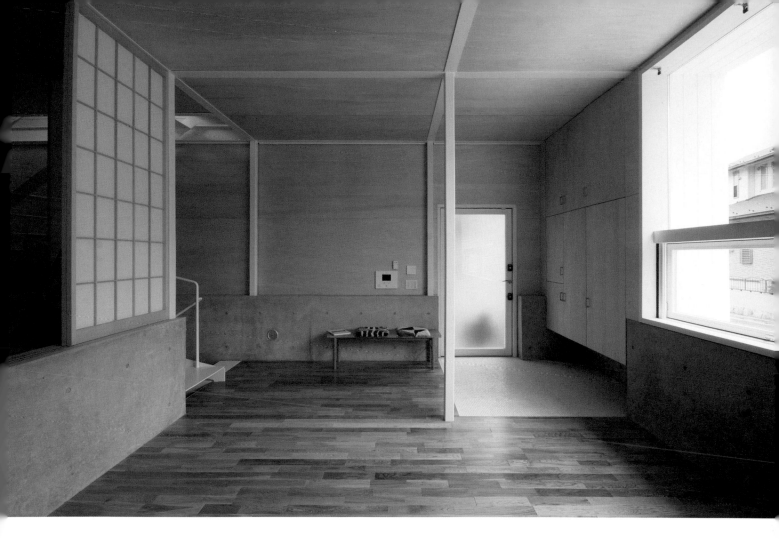

Inside the house, the architects employ a reasoned contrast of wood, concrete, glass, and steel. They employ screens similar to the *shōji* to bring together modernity and a clear reference to tradition.

Atelier Bow-Wow

Founded in 1992 by Yoshiharu Tsukamoto and Momoyo Kaijima, Atelier Bow–Wow has completed numerous private houses, but also such ambitious global projects as the BMW Guggenheim Lab (New York, 2010; Berlin, 2012).

www.bow-wow.jp

Interior spaces are sparsely furnished according to Japanese habit, allowing materials, light, and space to take center stage.

Steel, wood, and glass elements in the double-height spaces are carefully orchestrated to alternate with overhanging volumes.

A | Terrace
B | Living/Dining Room
C | Kitchen
D | Storage
E | Bedroom
F | Studio

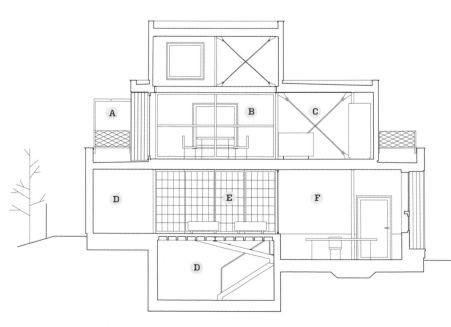

M House

Atelier Tekuto

LOCATION Tokyo

COMPLETED 2013

FLOOR AREA 720 ft²

SITE AREA 885 ft²

Like many clients in Tokyo, the owners of this house in the center of the city paid so much for the land that they had little left over for the construction budget. Describing their response to this constraint, the architects state, "Our main focus was to provide a spacious and open family space with sufficient natural light, where the family could comfortably spend most of their time." This family area on the upper floor includes a living and dining area, as well as the kitchen, and opens onto a balcony. The volume of this level projects outward to the street, with large windows set at its north and south ends. Additional fenestration under the single-slope roof brings in ample natural light, and wood floors and beams make the house a bit warmer than many Japanese residences from the outset. Perhaps because of the limited space usually available for private houses in an urban environment, furnishings and objects are kept to a strict minimum. The architects themselves say that the house was kept as "minimal and compact as possible," with bedrooms on the ground level. The trapezoidal lot includes just enough space for a car, with the rectangular volumes of the house occupying most of the plan area.

In the bright interior, wood floors
and beams contrast with white walls
and kitchen. An outdoor terrace,
with a wood floor like that inside,
offers extended space, light, and
fresh air during warmer months.

SECOND FLOOR

A | LDK
B | Balcony

FIRST FLOOR

C | Bathroom
D | Bedroom
E | Storage

M HOUSE   59

Monoclinic
Atelier Tekuto

LOCATION Tokyo

COMPLETED 2012

FLOOR AREA 980 ft²

SITE AREA 925 ft²

The architects find a solution to urban clutter in this unusual concrete building with generous geometric openings oriented to the sky. The polyhedron imposes its external angles and windows on the interior, whose levels and stairways echo the outer form.

Atelier Tekuto

Yasuhiro Yamashita was born in Kagoshima in 1960. He worked with Yutaka Saito Architect & Associates, PANOM, and Shunji Kondo Architects, before founding his own firm, Yamashita Kai Architectural Office, in 1991 in Tokyo. The firm was renamed Atelier Tekuto in 1995.

www.tekuto.com

In their concept for Monoclinic, conceived as a secondary house for clients in the residential area of Setagayaku, Tokyo, the architects set out to "design the sky." As they explain, "When designing a house in an urban context, surrounded by buildings, it is very important to think about the connection between architecture and the sky. The top plane of this polyhedron becomes a large skylight, connecting the living space with the sky." A large, angled square window, surrounded by four smaller triangular windows, is visible at the upper level from the street side. The living area ascends 18 feet and is generously filled with natural overhead light. A reinforced concrete building, Monoclinic includes two studio apartments for rent, and is angled back on the street side to provide a parking spot. A garage and "hobby room," as well as one rental bedroom with bath and kitchenette, are located at ground level. The second rental is located on the upper level, along with the bathroom, living space, and kitchen of the clients.

Interiors contrast opaque concrete surfaces with bright openings. Bathroom facilities are lodged in an open podium (this page). A light, sculptural stairway links the lower level to the generously glazed living space (opposite).

A | Living Room
B | Loft
C | Bathroom
D | Bedroom
E | Garage/Hobby Room

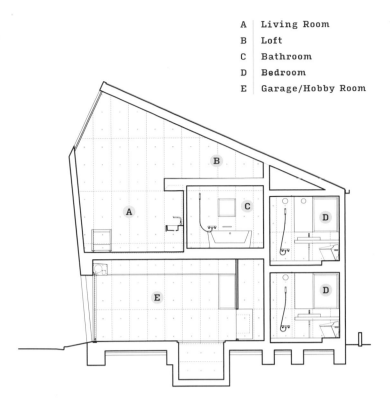

Villa in Sengokuhara
Shigeru Ban Architects

LOCATION Hakone, Kanagawa

COMPLETED 2013

FLOOR AREA 4,875 ft²

SITE AREA 19,050 ft²

SHIGERU BAN ARCHITECTS

Hakone is located in a mountainous area in the west of the Kanagawa Prefecture. It is known for its hot baths (*onsen*) and for such museums as the Hakone Open-Air Museum of Sculpture. In this rural setting is a two-story wooden residence with a partial steel structure and a large floor area. Shigeru Ban's unusual plan forms a generous central courtyard with a teardrop shape, 50 feet in diameter, around which the spaces of the house itself are arranged. Eight sliding doors separate the living room and the interior courtyard; when opened they provide free access to the outdoor space. The overhanging roof protects these doorways and the full-height glazing around the interior court. Wooden columns and beams are arranged in a radial pattern centered on the courtyard around the single-slope roof that varies in height between 8 and 25 feet above grade.

Inside, wood is omnipresent, from the roof beams, left completely exposed, to the vertical wooden posts arranged to form open walls or screens that give an overall impression of continuity throughout the interior space. A small mezzanine level is set below the highest point of the roof at one end of the structure. Shigeru Ban has worked on a number of large houses, in particular outside of Japan, and the Villa in Sengokuhara is particularly spacious by Japanese standards. Like many of Ban's works, it can be said here that the architect is deliberately experimenting, seeking to expand the boundaries of more traditional or typical design and construction.

Quite large by Japanese standards, the spiraling form of this house encloses a central green courtyard, providing both privacy and open views to the sky and greenery.

The wooden columns and beams covering the outer terrace are extended inside the house, giving both rhythm and movement to the spaces. Numerous spaces provide for a seamless transition from exterior to interior, particularly in warmer months. With this house, Shigeru Ban proves his capacity to innovate and to renew his architectural vocabulary.

Exploded
Axonometric

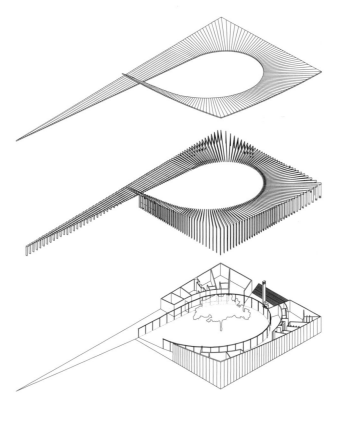

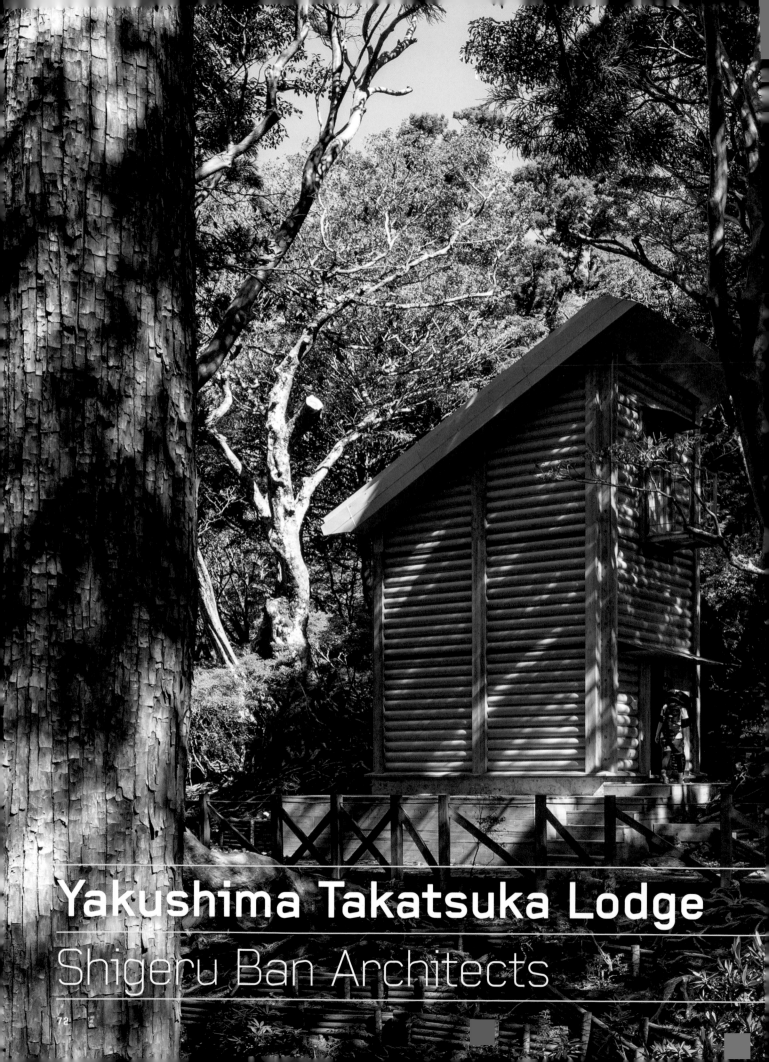

Yakushima Takatsuka Lodge

Shigeru Ban Architects

LOCATION   Yakushima, Kagoshima

COMPLETED   2013

FLOOR AREA 355 ft²

SITE AREA   N/A

SHIGERU BAN ARCHITECTS

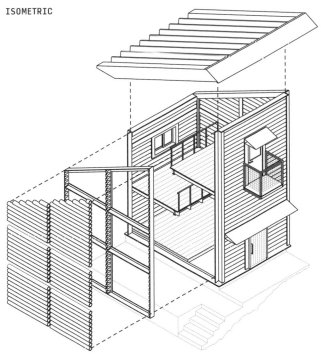

Not a residence but rather an "open house," this mountain hut serves as a refuge for anybody passing nearby. Located in the Kirishima–Yaku National Park on Yakushima Island, it was built on the foundations of an older structure that was in disrepair. Yakushima is about 40 miles south of Kyushu, in the extreme south of Japan, and a large area of the island was designated a Man and the Biosphere Reserve by UNESCO in 1980.

A relatively uncomplicated structure with a single-slope roof meant to quickly drain off rain, which is persistent on the island, the lodge has paper tube walls that alternate with transparent strips, allowing natural light to flood the interior. Given the relatively harsh environment of the structure's mountain setting, the architects emphasize that the paper tubes can be easily replaced if damaged. While this might not be considered a "house" in the sense of most of the other structures in this volume, the contrast between this extremely simple structure set in the woods and the very large Villa in Sengokuhara shows the range of the architect's talents. It emphasizes Ban's signature building unit, the recycled-paper tube, with which he has designed numerous projects, most notably for post-disaster contexts from Turkey to the Philippines. But his material vocabulary of wood, paper, metal, and light, and even its open interior, does not really differentiate the lodge from many Japanese houses. Instead, it is perhaps the sloped, densely wooded environment here that distinguishes this structure from the majority of houses in urban settings.

Shigeru Ban Architects

Shigeru Ban is the 2014 recipient of the Pritzker Architecture Prize. Born in 1957 in Tokyo, he gained worldwide attention for his innovative temporary shelters in disaster zones across the globe, starting with the region around Kobe after the devastating Hanshin earthquake of 1995. He continues to build in other practice areas, including the new Centre Pompidou–Metz (2010) and Aspen Museum (2014), as well as residences.

www.shigerubanarchitects.com

House SH / Hashira-ma

C+A Coelacanth and Associates

LOCATION   Tokyo

COMPLETED   2013

FLOOR AREA   700 ft²

SITE AREA   440 ft²

With a very limited site area, the
architects create a spacious interior
with high ceilings and natural
light playing off the light wood and
white interiors.

This three-story house with a steel structure is
located in the central Shibuya-ku area of Tokyo, near
where the architects are based. As is frequently the
case in this part of the Japanese capital, land is hard
to come by, and here the architects had to work within
a very small site area. They explain, "Even at the site's
maximum FAR, the floor area is less than 260 square
feet. We aimed at making the structure as light as
possible, due to the compactness of the site and the
narrowness of the front road, and at reducing the total
cost." The structure is made up of six central square
columns, each 2 inches wide, and light channel iron
braces, measuring 16 by 3 inches, on the periphery.

This central structure allows the architects to make thin,
non-load-bearing walls, increasing interior space.

A bedroom and bath are located on the first floor,
the living space and kitchen on the second floor, and
another room and balcony are on the top level. The
architects explain, "The ceiling is kept low and compact
for the first-floor bedroom and the third-floor study.
In contrast, the second-floor living/dining room, where
most of the time would be spent, has a comfortable
ceiling height of ten feet." Despite the narrowness of the
site, the architects included high windows to bring light
into the small residence.

No matter how tightly packed
Japanese houses may appear in urban
areas, there are no party walls to
mitigate the effects of earthquakes,
a constant preoccupation of
Japanese architects and engineers.

Materials and colors give a light, almost evanescent appearance to the interiors. Partitions and curtains are favored over interior walls where possible.

A curtain and a partial screen allow light in but provide for privacy.

In these two photos, a curtain is drawn or pulled back to partition space. As the plans show, there are few internal divisions.

THIRD FLOOR

A | Bedroom
B | Lavatory
C | Balcony

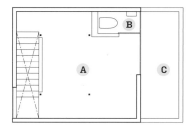

SECOND FLOOR

D | LDK

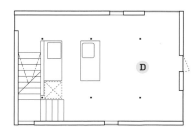

FIRST FLOOR

E | Lavatory
F | Bathroom
G | Bedroom

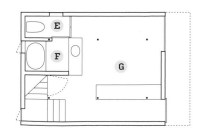

Memory of the Sky

C+A Coelacanth and Associates

LOCATION   Kamo, Gifu

COMPLETED   2010

FLOOR AREA 780 ft²

SITE AREA   4,550 ft²

This single-story wooden villa for the sculptor Takeshi Hayashi was built in a wooded, mountainous setting. The architects sought to create a number of "independent private spaces and a generous one-room space." "Many and one coexist," they say, "and the visible and invisible are contiguous in this space." The inspiration for the rounded triangular plan is the Japanese rice ball, or *omusubi*, arranged in "petals" around a courtyard. It is in this courtyard that the sculptor displays *Memories of Rain*, a work created to fit the shape of the courtyard. Despite its natural setting, the house, like many others in Japan, tends to appear closed from the outer periphery but is much more open within, absorbing ample natural light from the central courtyard. While the closure of the exterior surfaces of the house might seem to exclude nature from the inhabitants' experience, light, breeze, and nature in fact permeate the house. This inversion, or willful need to look at the sky, may be somewhat difficult to understand in Western eyes, but both the unusual reference to traditional rice balls in the plan and the very name of the residence are evidence that the architects have sought to integrate Japanese tradition into a very modern structure.

The exterior of the house gives an almost entirely closed impression, while an aerial view and courtyard images show how the house is made fully permeable to natural light and air.

C+A Coelacanth and Associates

C+A Coelacanth and Associates was formed in 2005 by Kazuko Akamatsu (b. 1968, Tokyo) and Kazuhiro Kojima (b. 1958, Osaka). The firm has worked on the Liberal Arts & Science College at Education City (Doha, Qatar, 2004, master plan Arata Isozaki, i-Net), and again with Isozaki on the Naryn campus of the University of Central Asia (Aga Khan Development Network, Kyrgyzstan, 2009).

www.c-and-a.co.jp

Interior views show narrow passages and smooth spatial transitions rather than closed volumes.

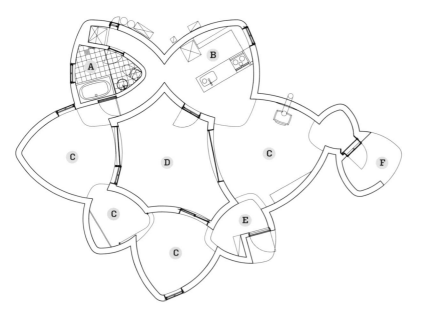

A	Bathroom
B	Kitchen
C	Bedroom
D	Courtyard
E	Entrance
F	Terrace

Nearly full-height glazing appears to make the outdoor courtyard part of the interior space of the house.

Curves and fenestration in unexpected locations (bottom left) emphasize the continuity of the volumes.

dNb

CO2Works

LOCATION Nagoya, Aichi

COMPLETED 2012

FLOOR AREA 2,875 ft²

SITE AREA 2,065 ft²

Formed with concrete slabs and a concrete facade that forms a kind of artificial "forest", the building is made up of two volumes with a ground-level difference of five feet from one street-facing side to the other.

With dNb (Daimancho Nakawatase Building), Koji
Nakawatase asks if architecture can be part of its
setting, just as "nature has its own characteristic
form and harmony within the environment." Nakawatase
completed his own home and office on a busy street in
the Daimancho area of Nagoya. The unusual reinforced
concrete building appears to be made up of a series of
tilting columns and floor plates arranged in a tree-like
pattern. Because of the 5-foot height difference from
one end of the site to the other, the architect determined
that it was necessary to create two interconnected
blocks. This height disparity is reflected in the half-
story difference between the floor levels of the
structure's two parts. To avoid the eventual instability
caused by tilted columns, Nakawatase "leaned" the
two volumes toward each other. Walls are arranged in a
"radial pattern from the center of the site." He says,
"Perhaps this system of mutual support is a metaphor for
plants huddling together as protection from the wind."

The "skipped floor" system, employed together with
cantilevered slabs, allows for good ventilation. Much
of the structure is in raw concrete, with some wood used
for floors or doors. This is dictated by the architect's
philosophy, according to which the interior and exterior
must be coherent not only with the urban environment,
but also with each other. Breeze enters the structure at
various points, as does a good deal of natural light—
manifestations of the Japanese interpretation of nature
and its presence, even within a dense city. The ground
floor of the building contains a hall, gallery, and
kitchen. The first floor has a living room and bedroom.
A library and offices are located on the second level.

A | Office
B | Living Room
C | Library
D | Bedroom
E | Hall

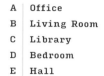

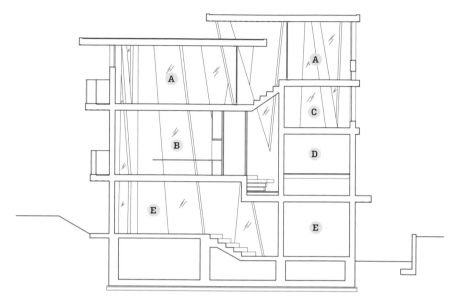

CO2Works

Koji Nakawatase (b. 1977) graduated from the Aichi Institute of Technology in 2000 and founded CO2Works in Nagoya in 2003.

www.co2works.com

Interiors have generous glazing between the tilted concrete surfaces that form the facade.

Wood used for furniture and some surfaces contrasts with the otherwise omnipresent concrete.

House in Nagohara

doubleNegatives Architecture

LOCATION   Minamimaki, Nagano

COMPLETED 2013

FLOOR AREA 915 ft²

SITE AREA 10,940 ft²

This vacation house has a steel frame and poured-in-place reinforced concrete roof. Essentially comprising a single room, it occupies a rather large site near the foothills of the Yatsugatake Mountains. The exterior is covered in oriented strand board (OSB), with a fluorocarbon polymer coating and generous glazing at ground level. The primary materials inside the house are painted steel, trowel finish mortar, and cedar. Windows are placed with respect to the topography of the site, while the kitchen, divided by a long, high table, is positioned at the intersection where the panoramic view opens up.

Further developing on their original approach to this project and their other work, the architects explain that the "two floors are connected to both the low and high sides of the site. The living space is linked to the site's shape physically and mentally, [and joins with its] expansive [character] as an extension beyond the floors." More prosaically, the house's low spiral form resembles a snail's shell.

The complexity suggested by this house's external forms is confirmed in its interior. Covered areas extend living space in clement weather.

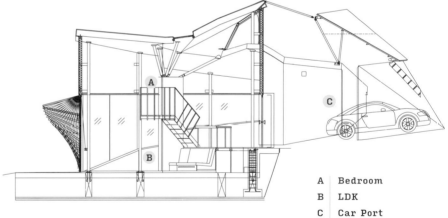

A | Bedroom
B | LDK
C | Car Port

doubleNegatives Architecture
Tokyo–based doubleNegatives Architecture is a group of architects, graphic designers, software programmers, and a musician, under the direction of Sota Ichikawa.

doublenegatives.jp

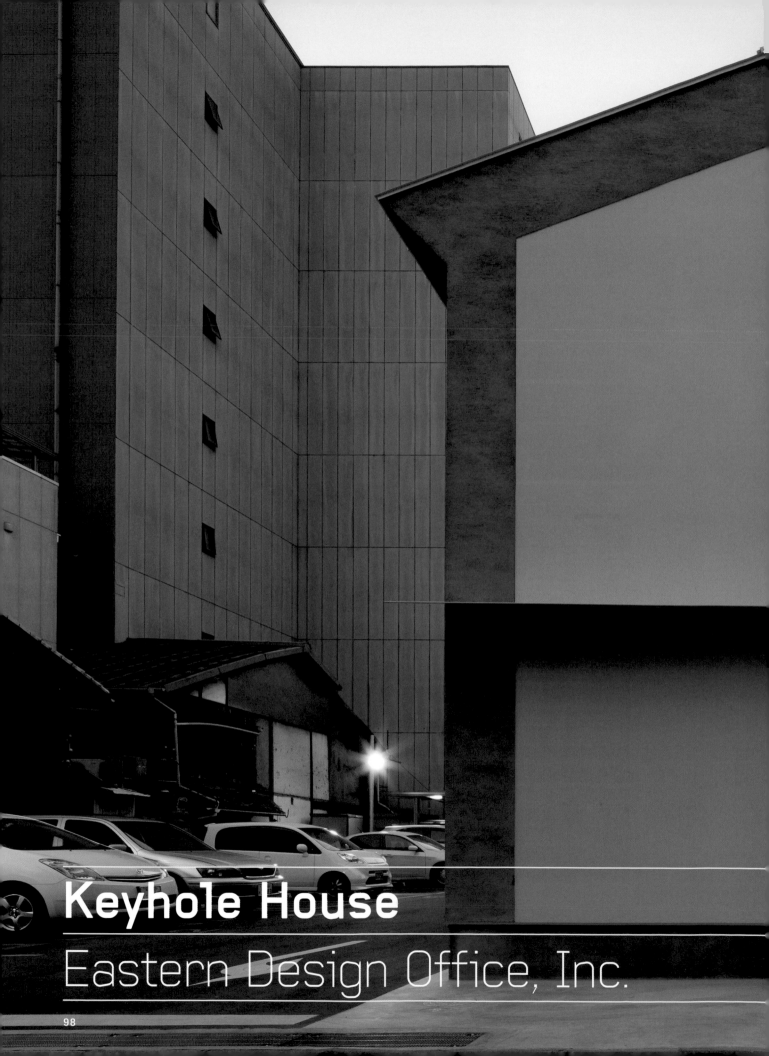

Keyhole House
Eastern Design Office, Inc.

LOCATION Kyoto

COMPLETED 2011

FLOOR AREA 1,110 ft²

SITE AREA 980 ft²

This house has a very limited floor area, given that it is intended for four inhabitants (and two cats). Fortunately, Eastern Design Office has made a strong local reputation with unusual houses, often in concrete, with unexpected forms and apertures. The rectangular house has a living, dining, and kitchen area on the ground floor, as well as a "Japanese style" room and a bath. A "catwalk" (for the cats) is installed on the upper wall of the living area. The upper floor has two bedrooms, a living space, and toilets, as well as a terrace. The house is entered from the east, its main facades almost precisely aligned on the east–west axis.

The bright purple entrance door is partially framed by a right–angle slit window that glows from within at night. A thin purple steel canopy marks the entrance facade, passing over the asymmetrically placed doorway. For the architects, "the facade of this house has the shape of a keyhole . . . A house can be called a key, which will open up your life happily." Exterior walls are finished in mortar with *sumi* ink (*sumi-e* is the art of Japanese brush painting), with windows appearing to be positioned randomly along the upper level, serving to bring ample light into the house; its street facade otherwise appears rather closed.

Eastern Design Office has often experimented with unique openings, cut-outs, or skylights in their residential designs. Unusual window placements that animate the volume are particularly striking at nightfall.

Eastern Design Office, Inc.
The principals of Eastern Design Office are Anna Nakamura, born in Osaka in 1974, and Taiyo Jinno, born in Aichi in 1968. They founded their firm in Kyoto in 2003.
www.easterndesignoffice.com

SECOND FLOOR

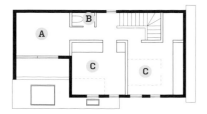

A | Living Room
B | Lavatory
C | Bedroom

FIRST FLOOR

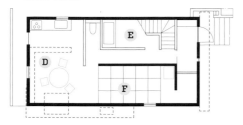

D | LDK
E | Bathroom
F | "Japanese Style" Room

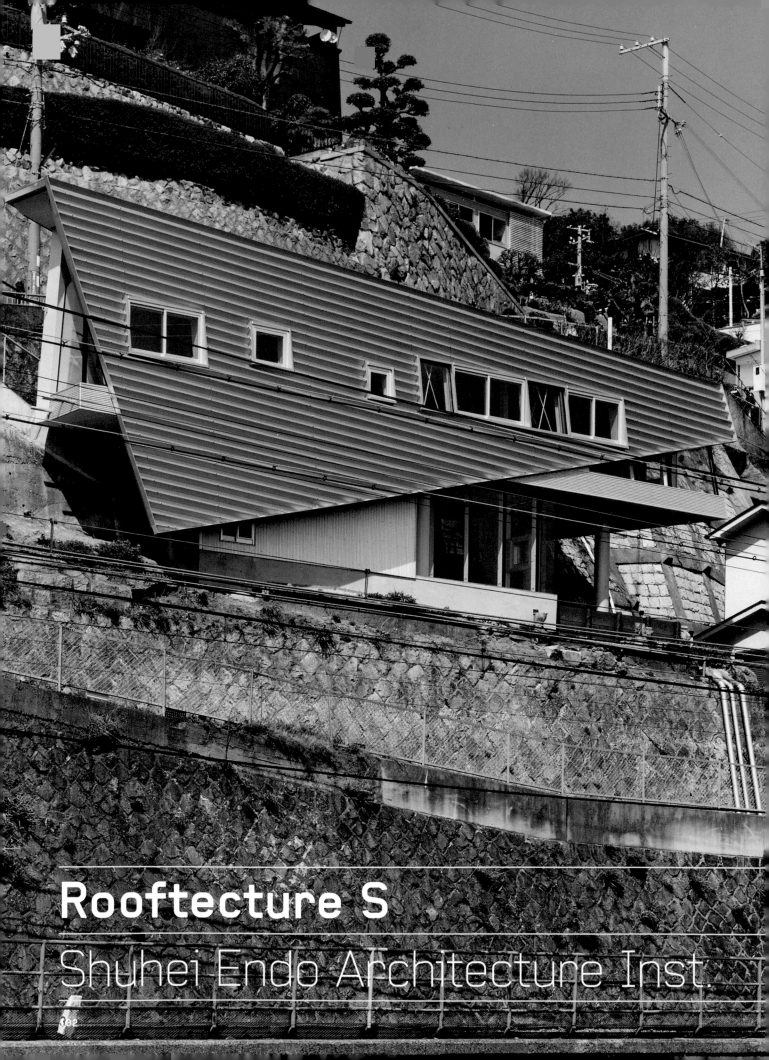

Rooftecture S
Shuhei Endo Architecture Inst.

LOCATION   Kobe, Hyogo

COMPLETED 2008

FLOOR AREA 720 ft²

SITE AREA 1,400 ft²

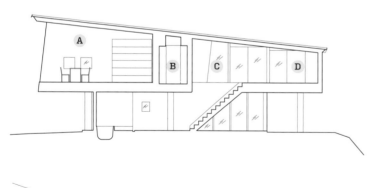

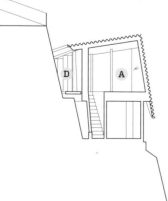

A | Dining/Kitchen Area
B | Entrance
C | Living Room
D | Terrace

Shuhei Endo Architecture Institute
Shuhei Endo was born in Shiga Prefecture. He worked with the architect Osamu Ishii and established his own firm in 1988.

www.paramodern.com

This steel-frame house is clad in galvanized steel sheet, but inside, plywood and wood flooring dominate. Located on a triangular site facing the Inland Sea of Japan, and sitting above railway tracks, the house adapts itself to the site, which is 65 feet long but varies in depth between only 5 and 13 feet. Due to the tiered platforms used to develop this residential area, the basic ground level is 16 to 26 feet lower than the entrance, further complicating the design. An "artificial ground" level was created on five piles. A narrow wooden terrace bridges the back of the house and a stone retaining wall.

"The development of the roof/wall is marked by rectangular sheet metal shingle boards. It maintains the logical forms pertaining to the slope and the triangular site by folding and tilting. States of liberation and enclosure created through the interaction with the slope," states architect Shuhei Endo, "define this house's spatial quality." The facade, which folds up to form a narrow roof, also develops the triangular form seen in the plan of the house. The artificial ground level of the house includes a covered terrace, while the main living areas, including the partially open bedroom, are on the upper level.

A small, difficult site is used to the utmost by the architect, who plays with the notion of a roof that folds to become the main facade. Interior views give a ship-like impression.

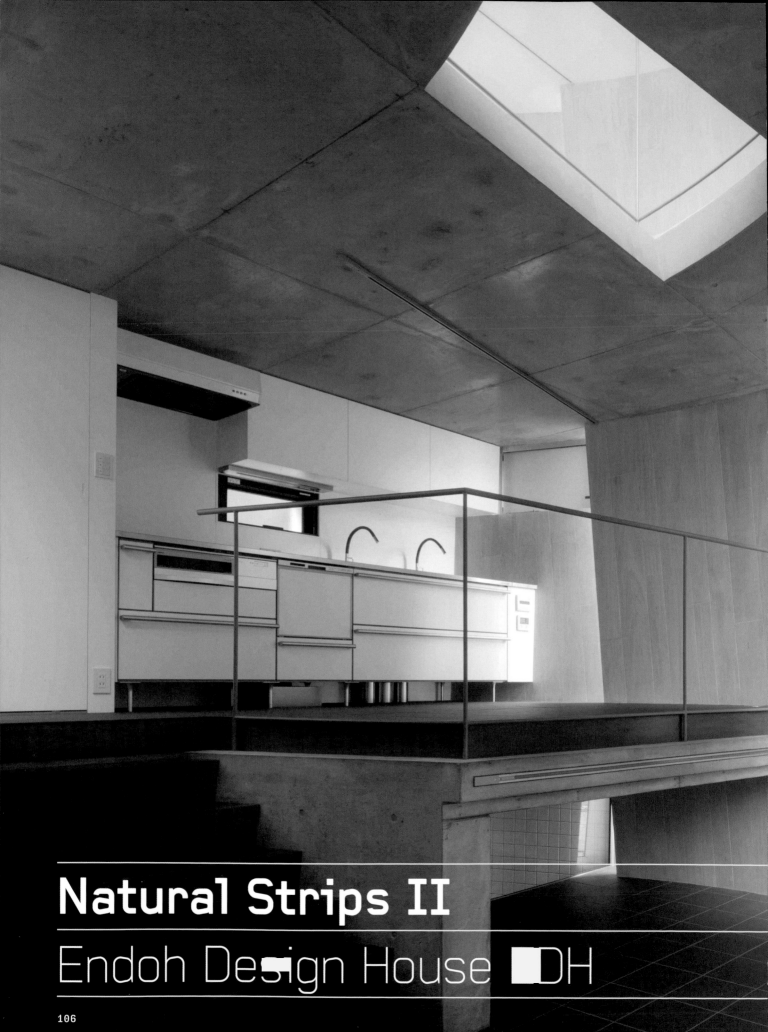

Natural Strips II

Endoh Design House ▮DH

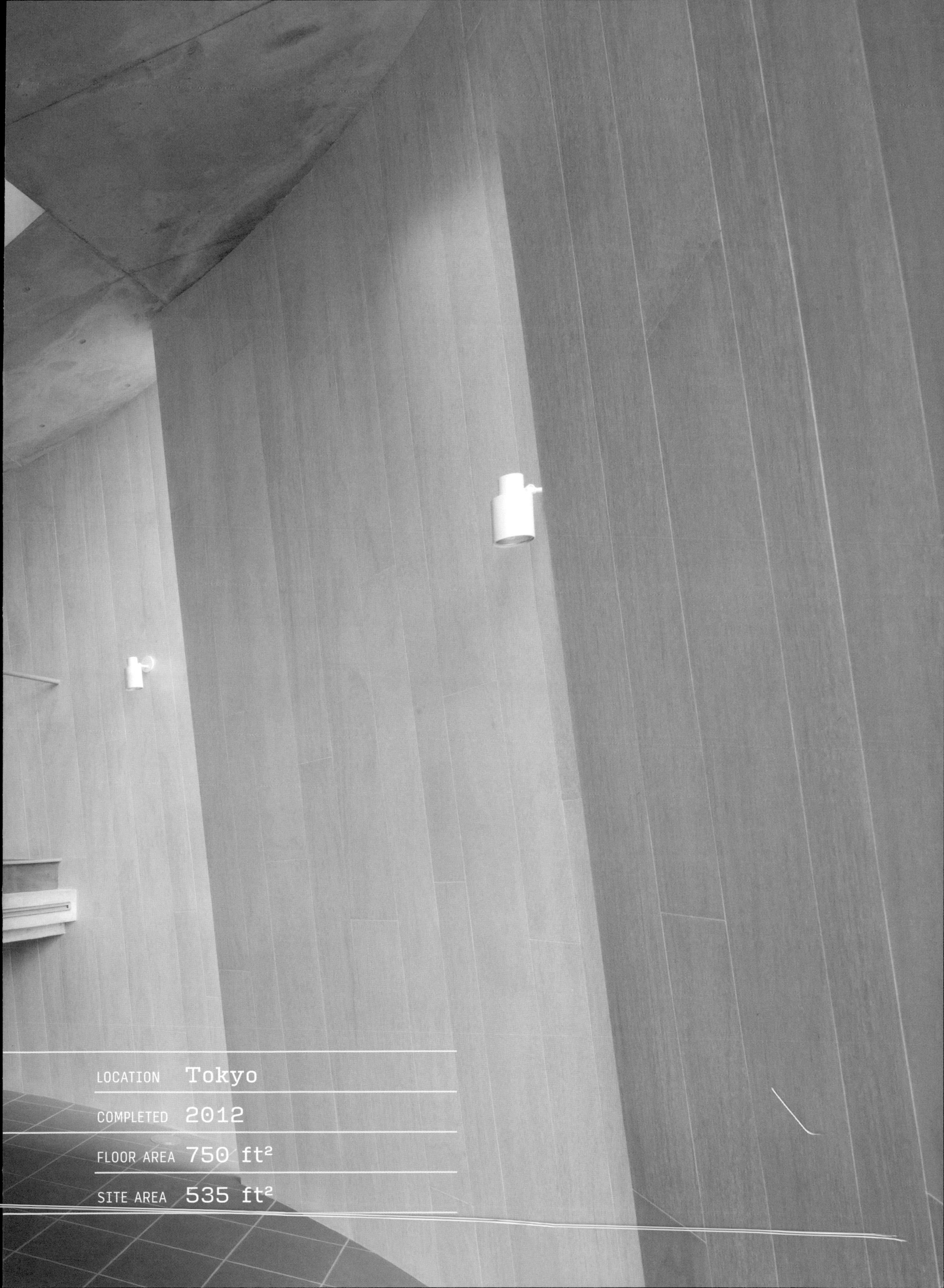

LOCATION   Tokyo

COMPLETED   2012

FLOOR AREA   750 ft²

SITE AREA   535 ft²

A Children's Room
B Terrace
C Kitchen
D Living Room
E Bathroom
F Car Port
G Master Bedroom

This three-level house for a family of four is located on a very small site in the central Shibuya area of Tokyo. The master bedroom is located in the basement, and the first level includes a carport and the entrance area created by an opening in the exterior walls. Just above the entrance, a bathroom is inserted to save space. The second floor has a high-ceilinged living room with the kitchen perched above the lower-level bathroom. The third floor has a children's bedroom, a loft, and a terrace.

The architect explains "Most of the houses in the neighborhood are only two stories; the third-floor terrace provides a sense of wide open space, as well as a view overlooking the neighborhood." On the street side, the curving main facade of the house is made up of four overlapping segments of steel frames and cement, clad in plywood on the interior. The overlapping walls create high slit windows, which allow natural light into the house without giving up its privacy. The color palette is muted throughout. The architect states, "The walls are painted a pale white to brighten the room while allowing the wood grain to show through. The concrete ceiling matches the gray tile floor." An L-shaped concrete wall closes the back of the structure.

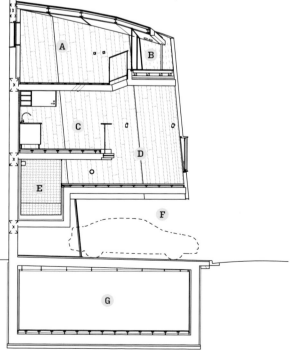

The unusual exterior form of the structure takes into account a frequent feature of Japanese urban homes: a covered, ground level parking spot. Inside spaces are folded and curved to take full advantage of the shape of the building.

Natural Sticks II
Endoh Design House EDH

LOCATION   Tokyo

COMPLETED   2012

FLOOR AREA   2,280 ft²

SITE AREA   1,160 ft²

ENDOH DESIGN HOUSE EDH

A screen form, somewhat reminiscent of a folding fan, characterizes the main facade. Its curvature creates the space for a covered parking area.

Interested in structural innovation, Masaki Endoh designed this house with a flat rear wall and a series of standard "I" columns "arranged in fan shapes to create curved walls that maximize available space." A garage, open-air parking space, and carport, above which the living room is set, are part of the scheme. A large staircase connects the basement to the first and second floors, as does an elevator; the frame of this connected space doubles as shelving for books and the owner's collection of shoes worn by famous athletes. The second-floor LDK area has a full-height window, with a children's room on the upper level and a terrace above the living room. As in Natural Strips II, the main bedroom is in the basement. Behind and below the carport there is an outdoor space, covered in wire-mesh, which can be used as a garden. There are two storage areas in the rear part of the basement, one of which may be converted into a bedroom. The architect states, "The steel 'I' columns make curved walls possible in modern architecture. Normally, standard building materials in Japan today only allow for flat walls. By using a modern material with traditional shapes and a different approach, new possibilities open up, both practically and esthetically."

ENDOH DESIGN HOUSE EDH

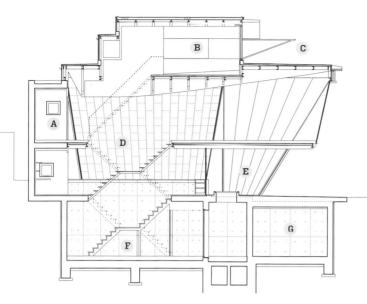

A | Bathroom
B | Bedroom
C | Terrace
D | Living Room
E | Parking
F | Storage
G | Main Bedroom and
    Service Areas

Wall space is almost fully occupied by shelves for books or objects, while the kitchen appears to hover in equilibrium above the lower level. Plunging, curved surfaces correspond to the exterior envelope in their inspiration.

Endoh Design House EDH
Masaki Endoh was born in Tokyo in 1963 and established his firm in 1994.

www.edh-web.com/

Hamamatsu House
Terunobu Fujimori

LOCATION   Hamamatsu,Shizuoka

COMPLETED 2012

FLOOR AREA 2,710 ft²

SITE AREA 4,210 ft²

Terunobu Fujimori
Terunobu Fujimori (b. 1946) is a
Professor Emeritus at the University
of Tokyo's Institute of Industrial
Science. Although his main activity
is devoted to research on Western-
style buildings in Japan from
the Meiji period through the modern
era, he is also a practicing
architect.

Terunobu Fujimori began his career as a professor specializing in Western-style edifices built in Japan from the Meiji period onward. "I didn't start designing buildings until my forties, so the condition I set for myself is that I shouldn't just repeat the same things that my colleagues or professors were doing," he has stated. His often quirky buildings clearly call on his extensive knowledge of Japanese architectural tradition. In the case of the Hamamatsu House, Fujimori sought to combine traditional and modern ideas in features such as the zinc-coated iron fireplace or the FRP (Fiber Reinforced Plastic) lampshades. He is interested in designs in which he can control not only the exterior appearance of the architecture, but also its interior architecture and décor. With its charred black wood exterior and wooden details, the two-story house certainly gives the impression of being traditionally inspired, but the space and sometimes unexpected use of forms gives it a very contemporary look. The ground floor includes a large "showroom and garage," the entrance, living and dining space, a kitchen, and a "Japanese Style room." The small second floor has a bedroom and bathroom. The architect's sense of humor can be seen with the small trees at the highest points of the roof, or the tree-like columns supporting the entrance canopy.

The wooden interior volumes of the house are at once in keeping with Japanese traditions and also modern in their conception and forms, such as the stairway or the hanging light fixtures.

A | Loft
B | Bedroom
C | Entrance
D | "Japanese Style" Room

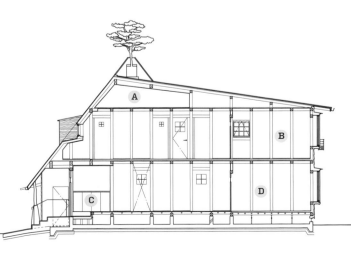

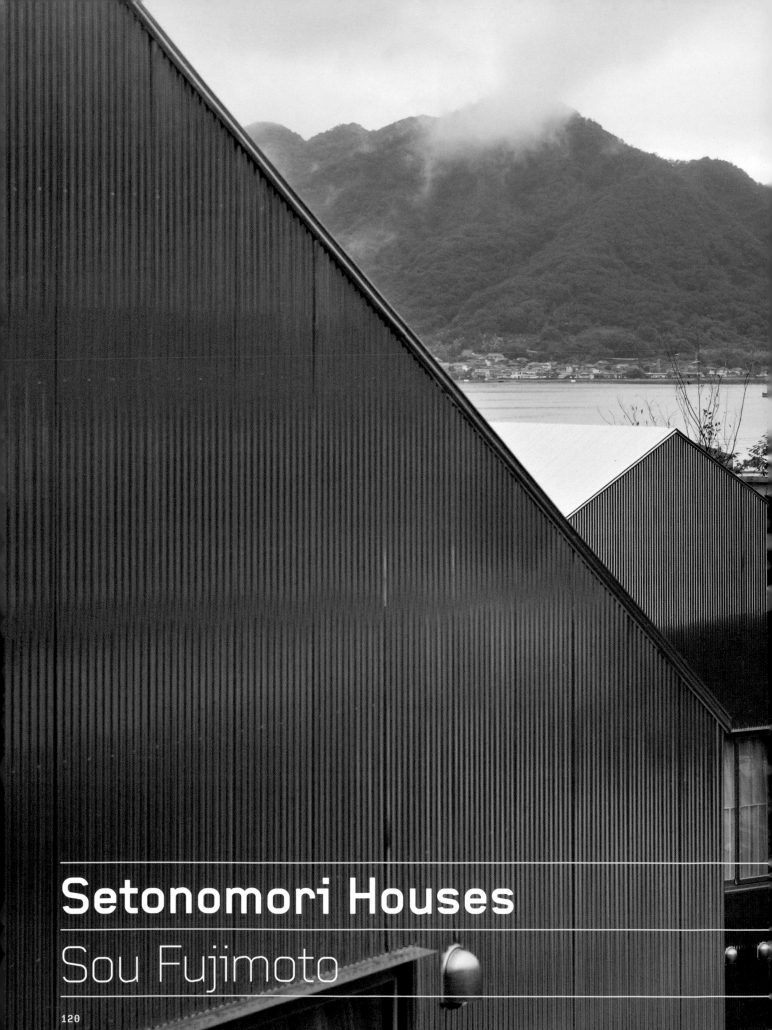

Setonomori Houses

Sou Fujimoto

LOCATION   Setouchi, Okayama

COMPLETED 2013

FLOOR AREA 19,720 m² (COMBINED)

SITE AREA 58,870 m²

The Setonomori Housing complex consists of 13 units, each forming two symmetrical houses, built on a slope between wooded mountains and the Inland Sea. Steep paths and stairways linked the existing structures on this coastal site, and the architect wondered how he might make use of this unusual configuration. "I had the feeling that it would turn into something unintentional yet new," says Sou Fujimoto. The scheme was conceived by careful adjustment of the volumes in relation to the existing topography, and more than 100 trees were planted after construction to "recreate the landscape," which had been ruined by a parking lot. Within the complex, the architect randomly placed fixtures such as frames for drying clothes, handrails, and stairs, as well as outside storage spaces. "It was not considered an abstract arrangement based on the symbolic house-shaped unit," he says, "but was intended to generate a 'living environment' by distributing various things in various ways." Covered in narrow, mirror-finished stainless steel plates, the houses quite literally reflect the changing seasons and the light of each day. "I hope people who live here will appreciate the flow of time in the ever-changing appearance of their houses," says Fujimoto. "Their memory will become a landscape and will be passed down to the future."

Despite their modern design, the gable-roofed houses are integrated into the site in such a way as to resemble older, more traditional Japanese residences. The basic floor plans are square.

A   Storage
B   Bathroom
C   Lavatory
D   Entrance
E   Kitchen
F   Living/Dining Room
G   Bedroom

FIRST FLOOR

SECOND FLOOR

Sou Fujimoto Architects

Sou Fujimoto (b. 1971) is clearly amongst the rising generation of Japanese architects who are seeking to innovate in both esthetic and structural terms. Winner of the 2012 Golden Lion (Best National Participation) for his design of the Japanese Pavilion exhibition at the Architecture Biennale in Venice, he also designed the 2013 Serpentine Summer Pavilion (Kensington Gardens, London, 2013).

www.sou-fujimoto.net

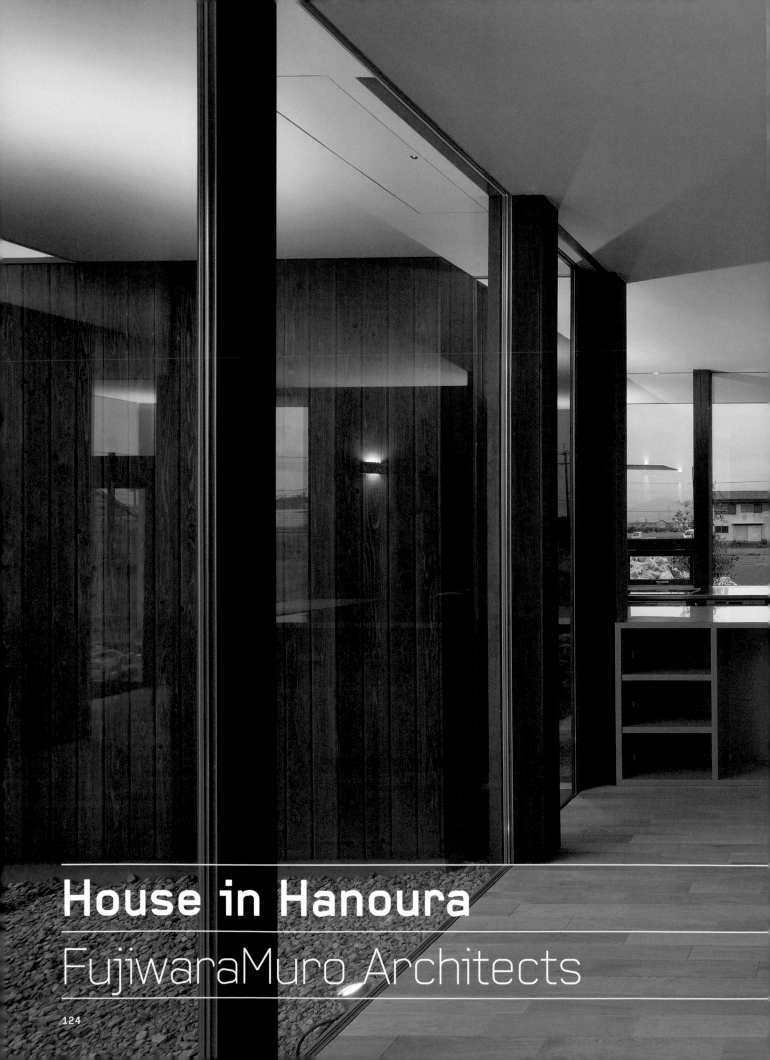

House in Hanoura

FujiwaraMuro Architects

LOCATION Hanoura, Tokushima

COMPLETED 2013

FLOOR AREA 1,020 ft²

SITE AREA 3,585 ft²

This house is on Shikoku Island, the least populated of the four main islands of Japan, noted for its stone-sculpting traditions.

This single-family house with a timber structure is located in a rural part of Tokushima Prefecture, on the island of Shikoku. The client asked that the residence be connected to the exterior. Since the site is isolated, there are few passersby, which made the request for a "liberated atmosphere" all the easier to accept. "Based on this," state the architects, "we decided to suggest a design in which you can feel the changes from moment to moment as the landscape changes throughout the year. On the site, the breeze can be felt from many directions, so we also wanted to make use of the wind flow." The designers started by imagining a series of small "hills" made of stones and sand. The irregularity of these piles of stone contrasts markedly with the rectilinear and rather "smooth" aspect of the architectural design. "By creating hills, we were able to give depth perception to the landscape so that, from within looking out, one sees hills in the foreground, rice fields beyond, and the sky above," they explain. Family life is centered around the living-dining-kitchen area, where breezes can pass through and the landscape can be seen on all sides. Individual rooms are arranged like pavilions around this central space. The living area is illuminated from the exterior at night, giving the impression that the roof is floating above the neighboring rice fields.

Wood surfaces contrast with modern kitchen elements, while full-height glazing brings in natural light and emphasizes continuity with the exterior.

A	Storage	E	Dining Room
B	Bathroom	F	Kitchen
C	Children's Room	G	Master Bedroom
D	Living Room	H	Entrance

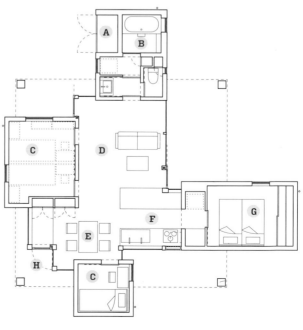

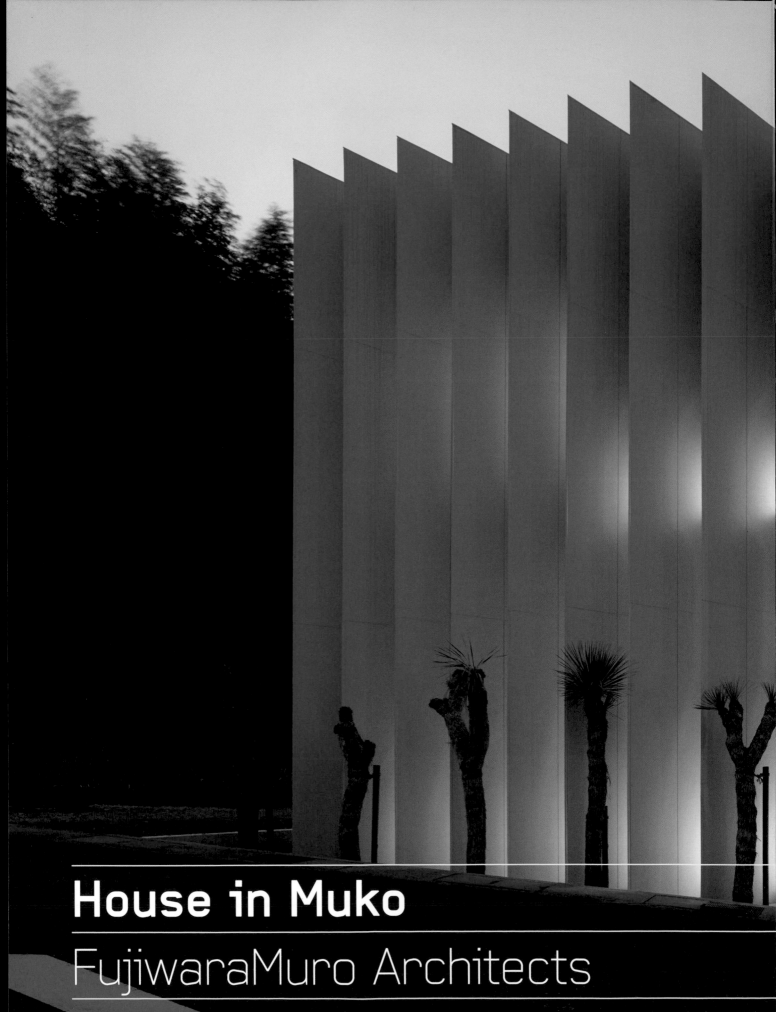

House in Muko

FujiwaraMuro Architects

LOCATION **Muko, Kyoto**

COMPLETED **2012**

FLOOR AREA **1,075 ft²**

SITE AREA **3,185 ft²**

While the architects refer to Japanese tradition, the house has a very modern appearance, using its louvers both as an element of visual identity and also filtering daylight and both inward and outward views. A gentle combination of wooden surfaces and furniture (opposite) sits against the background of the white louvers that penetrate the interior space.

Although this house is not far from the more traditional areas of Kyoto, it is actually in a newly developed residential zone. Located at the top of a hill, the site is shaped like a fan, with roads bordering the southern and eastern sides, and a bamboo grove to the west. The owner imagined that the unusual shape of the site would allow for the creation of an "interesting structure." Aside from this desire, he requested that the interior should form a continuous space with no partitions.

With no other structures bordering the site except to the north, the architects chose to make natural light and the movement of the sun part of their design. Thirteen 25-foot-tall vertical louvers are located on the south side of the building, blocking the line of sight from the road and bringing light into the house. The architects explain that the "design has similarities with the trellises found on the facades of merchant houses in Kyoto, and also brings to mind traditional Japanese sliding paper partitions" (*shoji*). Lights placed on the inside of the louvers allow the house to be lit simultaneously inside and out. Mexican Yucca rostrata plants line the south side of the house. The split-level living space includes a kitchen, dining room, living room, and bedroom on the first floor. Structural pillars are incorporated in the kitchen as inconspicuously as possible. A playroom, study, and washroom form the lower part of the second floor, with a bathroom on the upper part and a rooftop deck above. The wood structure is covered in FRC (Fiber Reinforced Concrete) siding with a metal roof, and the interior is floored in oak. Despite the high price of these materials, their efficient use in the house means that the total cost was only ¥26,000,000 (approximately U.S. $250,000).

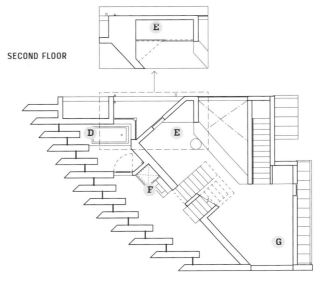

The louvers give rhythm and variety to the interior spaces, setting the pace of the views as the lighting conditions change naturally with the movement of the sun. Although white surfaces abound, the house seems "warmer" than many contemporary Japanese residences.

FujiwaraMuro Architects
Osaka-based FujiwaraMuro Architects was founded by principals Shintaro Fujiwara (b. 1974, Osaka), and Yoshio Muro (b. 1974, Nagoya) in 2002.

www.aplan.jp

FIRST FLOOR

SECOND FLOOR

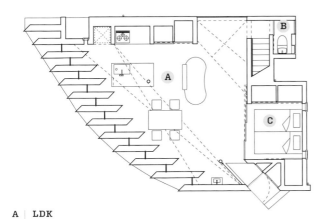

A | LDK
B | Lavatory
C | Bedroom

D | Bathroom
E | Children's Room
F | Lavatory
G | Children's Room

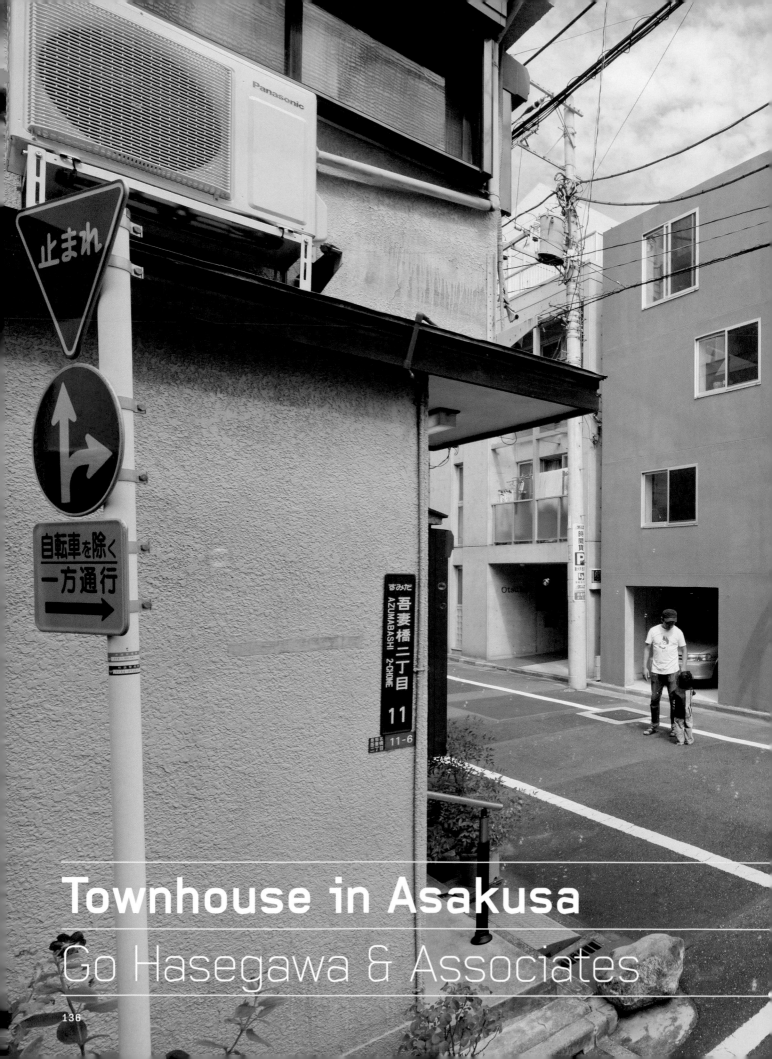

止まれ

自転車を除く
一方通行
→

すみだ
吾妻橋二丁目
AZUMABASHI
2-CHOME
11
11-6

Townhouse in Asakusa
Go Hasegawa & Associates

LOCATION   Tokyo

COMPLETED   2010

FLOOR AREA   1,230 ft²

SITE AREA   690 ft²

Window placement as seen from the exterior does not reveal the bright concrete interior within, nor is the sheltered rooftop terrace, partially occupied by a skylight, visible from the street.

Located in the densely populated, somewhat traditional Sumida Ward of Tokyo, this reinforced concrete townhouse has four stories, whereas most surrounding structures are generally three stories high. Go Hasegawa explains, "The ceiling height of each floor is 6 feet, but to eliminate any sense of discomfort, I made holes in the floor of each level. In some cases, this meant creating a huge opening in the center, and in others, I gave the floor a constricted form by making two more holes there. The large apertures create areas of light and shadow in various places on the same level as well as on the floor below, while also unifying the entire space. Moreover, due to the holes and the windows in the exterior walls, and by altering the position of the skylights, you can look down diagonally at the neighborhood from the upper floors, and look up at the windows from the lower floors." The openings in the floors are substantial enough to give the impression that the entire space is interconnected, and living areas resemble mini balconies or mezzanines. The rather austere gray rectilinear form of the house stands out in comparison to its neighbors.

The house assumes an almost kaleidoscopic variety of spaces, where stairways and mezzanines abound, creating an open and friendly atmosphere.

Go Hasegawa & Associates
Go Hasegawa, born in 1977 in Saitama, is another rising star of contemporary Japanese architecture. He worked in the office of Taira Nishizawa before creating Go Hasegawa & Associates in 2005.

www.hsgwg.com

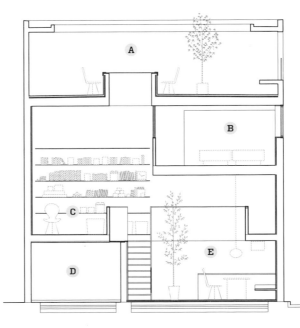

A	Terrace
B	Study
C	Play Room
D	Garage
E	Living Room

House in Komazawa

Go Hasegawa & Associates

LOCATION Tokyo

COMPLETED 2011

FLOOR AREA 690 ft²

SITE AREA 710 ft²

The total floor area of this two-story timber-frame house built in the Setagaya area of Tokyo, a calm residential district that features a mixture of detached houses and low-rise condominiums, is only slightly greater than its site area. The east side of the lot borders a grove of plum trees. Though adopting the gabled roof design that is common in the district, the architect decided to "restructure the relationship between the first and second floor." The first floor was raised and paved with small granite stones, like an outside patio. Go Hasegawa explains, "The rough space allows the residents to arrange their furniture and plants as they see fit on the stone-lined floor, and the open living room ensures a view out to the plum grove through a big window." The second floor has a plywood-lined bedroom and bath, but also a study with an unusual louvered floor. A high window on the second floor actually allows those on the ground to see the sky through the louvered floor surface.

"In this project," says Hasegawa, "I sensed a need for a contrast between the two floors (the light and expanse that is visible overhead from the first floor and the public atmosphere that you sense underfoot while on the second) that would create a mutually appealing environment."

Despite its simple square plan, this house reveals surprising internal volumes, especially given its unusual open wooden floor.

GO HASEGAWA & ASSOCIATES

GO HASEGAWA & ASSOCIATES

Japanese houses are voluntarily ambivalent, situated between infinite space and the reality of the dense cities of today: here, the courtyard is at once open to the sky, the breeze, and a controlled expression of nature, while remaining closed to the often chaotic urban environment.

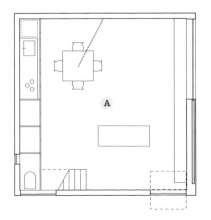

FIRST FLOOR

SECOND FLOOR

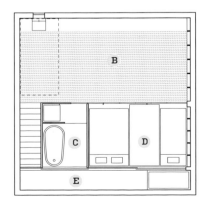

A | LDK
B | Study
C | Bathroom
D | Bedroom
E | Balcony

HOUSE IN KOMAZAWA   **147**

House in Kyodo

Go Hasegawa & Associates

LOCATION **Tokyo**

COMPLETED **2011**

FLOOR AREA **730 ft²**

SITE AREA **785 ft²**

The House in Kyodo is a two-story rectangular plan timber-frame house for a couple of editors in the Setagaya area of Tokyo. Given the couple's profession, the architect decided to make the entire first floor into a "book vault" and inserted a bathroom, entrance, study, bedroom, and closets in the gaps between the shelves. Intending to create a close, even physical relationship with the books, the design limits ceiling height on this level to a scant six feet. The upper-floor living room and terrace are considerably more voluminous. The division of space made apparent by the architect is also very much in the mind of the owners who decided that books would be kept exclusively on the ground floor, leaving the bright open space above free of the printed word. The roof is made with 2.3-inch steel sandwich panels, whose silvery underside reflects light and greenery from a neighboring garden. The form of the house may be traditional, but its layout is not, nor indeed is its appearance as seen from the street, where it is essentially blank, or from the sides, with generous fenestration, especially with the partial walls on the upper level.

GO HASEGAWA & ASSOCIATES

A | Kitchen
B | Living Room
C | Terrace
D | Bathroom
E | Study
F | Bedroom
G | Closet

Seen from the street, especially
with its sliding shutters in
the open position, the house looks
almost like a warehouse or store.
The narrow but airy upper level
living area is marked by the sloped
roof and large windows.

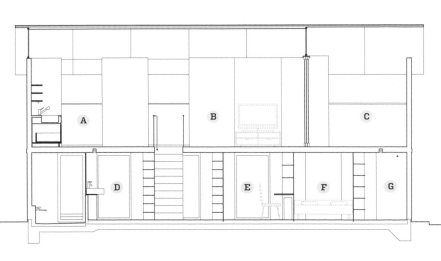

House in Mayu
Horibe Associates

LOCATION **Kishiwada, Osaka**

COMPLETED **2013**

FLOOR AREA **4,835 ft²**

SITE AREA **1,520 ft²**

Intended for a young couple with a child, this rectangular-plan residence features a Japanese-style combined kitchen, living, and dining area on one side and the bedroom and study on the other, with three square courtyards punctuating the outer periphery. These courtyards are intended to ensure privacy even if homes are built on surrounding lots in the future. Of the brief for this single-story wooden structure, Naoko Horibe explains, "The client requested a design that would melt into the surrounding rice paddy landscape, as well as provide a safe, stable living environment for generations to come." The architect goes on to explain that if two generations with different schedules eventually share the home, the courtyards will provide "a comfortable degree of distance between the living spaces occupied by various members of the household." Despite its relatively agricultural setting, the house appears to be largely closed when viewed from the exterior, but is more open within, with daylight penetrating from the courtyards.

Horibe Associates
Naoko Horibe was born in 1972 in Osaka. She graduated from Kinki University, Faculty of Science and Engineering (1995) then worked for Akira Sakamoto (CASA) and K. Associates/Architects before founding her own office in 2003.

horibeassociates.com

A	Approach
B	Lavatory
C	Washroom
D	Bathroom
E	Courtyard
F	Study
G	Free Space
H	Entrance
I	Closet
J	LDK
K	Closet
L	Bedroom
M	Tatami
N	Free Space

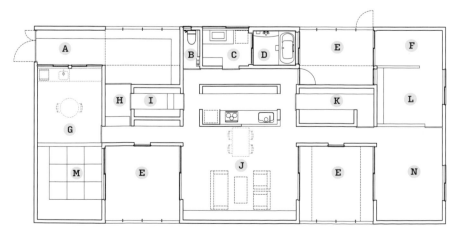

The house features three partially enclosed courtyards that bring air, natural light, and small trees into the otherwise orthogonal design. Typically, it is not views of the environment that are the architect's priority, but rather this gesture of bringing nature into the residence.

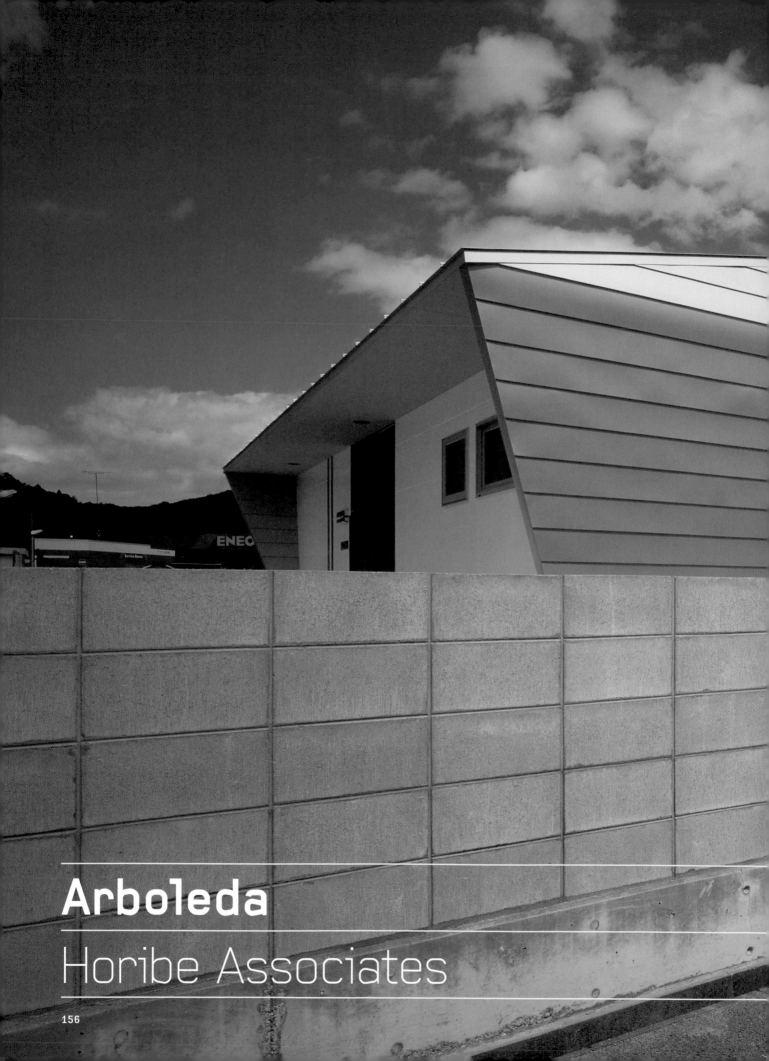

Arboleda
Horibe Associates

LOCATION   Anan, Tokushima

COMPLETED   2013

FLOOR AREA 810 ft²

SITE AREA   3,155 ft²

Located not far from Hanoura, where Fujiwaramuro Architects also built a residence (page 124), this is a single-story wood house for a couple with a child. As Naoko Horibe explains, "The client came to us with a request to combine two completely opposing concepts in a single structure, without a sense of clashing. One was an exterior that resembles a sports car; the second was a natural timber interior." All the rooms in the square-plan house are directly accessible from the central LDK area. The owner's den, in an elevated loft space, is furnished with an automobile seat by the famed German firm Recaro, which makes seats for Alfa Romeo, Ferrari, and Fiat, amongst others. A wrap-around metal cladding and upper triangular window that opens into the loft give a modern "sports car" appearance to the house. The name of the house, "Arboleda" means "grove" in Spanish. According to the architect, "this reflects both the radical exterior design's homage to Italian sports cars, and the interior's warm atmosphere, fashioned from wood."

LONG SECTION

A | Entrance
B | LDK
C | Bedroom

CROSS SECTION

D | LDK
E | Loft
F | Terrace

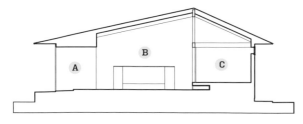

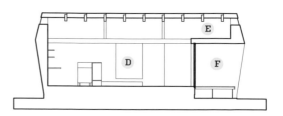

Despite the unusual appearance of this house's exterior, the interior conveys a much more traditional impression, with wood dominating on floors and ceilings. Light enters through the triangular windows under the eaves but also through a fully glazed facade.

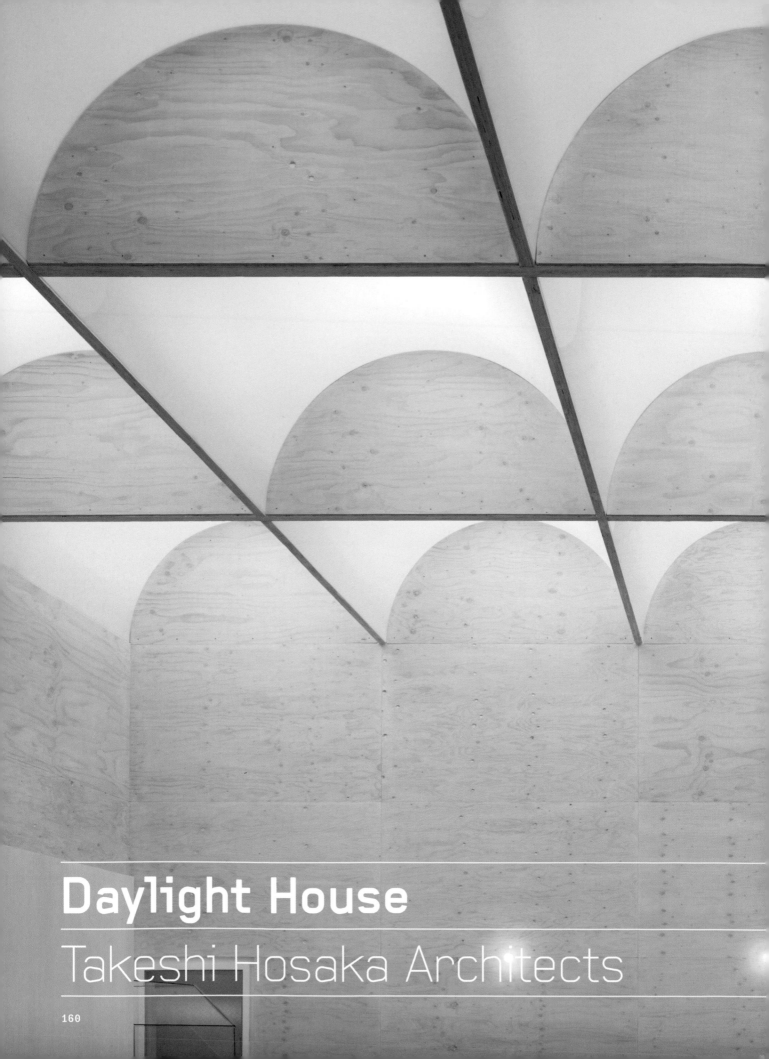

Daylight House
Takeshi Hosaka Architects

LOCATION **Yokohama, Kanagawa**

COMPLETED **2011**

FLOOR AREA **915 ft²**

SITE AREA **1,240 ft²**

Built for a couple and their two children, the Daylight House is set in a densely built area, close to the Yokohama railway station, that includes high-rise residential towers and offices as well as private houses. An unusual feature of the site is that the ground level is 10 feet below the road it is set on, meaning that natural light was at a premium from the outset. The architect responded to this challenge with a nearly 18-foot-high flat-roofed, metal-clad box that essentially forms a single room with a high ceiling. The master bedroom, children's rooms, and study are divided by doors and furniture about half the height of the ceiling. Because the system of high-set windows initially chosen by the architect would have made the entire interior of the house visible from the higher neighboring buildings, Hosaka decided to place an acrylic vault ceiling beneath these openings. A mortar floor and larch plywood walls are in harmony with the detailing of the white acrylic, "annihilating the very materiality of the surfaces." Although the house appears to be in a dimly lit site, this device allows the interior to be flooded with indirect light that changes in tonality and color at every hour of the day. Each room has a 35 x 27 inch window intended in part to allow air to circulate throughout the house.

TAKESHI HOSAKA ARCHITECTS

Faced with the problem of exterior
urban density, the architect has
created a calm, naturally lit space
beneath a skylight ceiling, bringing
to mind the words of Louis Kahn,
"No space, architecturally, is
a space unless it has natural light."

FIRST FLOOR

A | Entrance   E | Study
B | LDK   F | Closet
C | Bedroom   G | Bathroom
D | Lavatory

SECOND FLOOR

H | Balcony
I | Loft

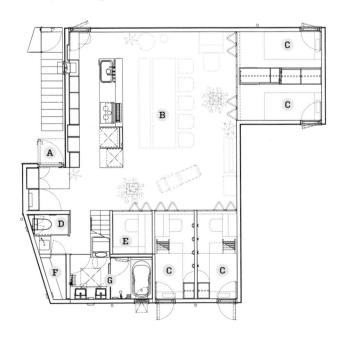

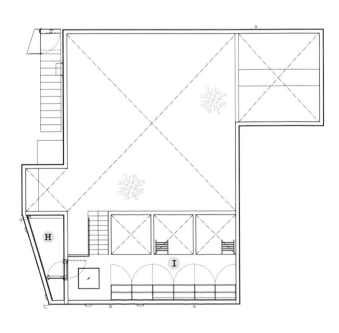

Squeezed into its dense urban
residential area, the house stands
out because of its vertical metal
cladding and its array of skylights,
as seen from above.

House in Byoubugaura
Takeshi Hosaka Architects

LOCATION   Yokohama, Kanagawa

COMPLETED 2012

FLOOR AREA 980 ft²

SITE AREA 700 ft²

This entire design was based on bringing breeze and
light into what appeared to be a terribly enclosed site.
Intended for a young couple with two children, the House
in Byoubugaura has a basement and two levels above
grade, each of equal height, for an overall height of 18
feet. Close to existing buildings on the south and north
sides, the site faces a 10-foot-high retaining wall to the
rear (east) of the site. Sliding windows were placed in
an alignment that gives the impression that the house is
three-stories high. Entrance, living, dining, and kitchen
areas are located on the rectangular-plan ground floor.
A spiral staircase leads to a bedroom and bath above.

In this unusual configuration, the exterior concrete
walls curve up, as do the interior wood floors, creating
the high band openings that characterize the facade.
Thanks to this gesture, windows at the rear don't look
onto the retaining wall, but instead are turned up to
the green hill behind. This house, which appears to
be rigorously orthogonal from the exterior, stands out
against neighboring buildings in the more "traditional"
Japanese residential style. In fact, the rectilinear plan
and the orthogonal appearance of the structure can only
be understood by looking at the architect's section
drawings. There are more curves inside this house than
anyone seeing it from the exterior might suspect.

The curved concrete volumes visible from the street serve both to assure privacy and to bring in light and air, especially to the lower floor, which is in fact below grade. Inside, an elegant combination of concrete, wood flooring, and light metal fixtures prevails.

LOCATION Sapporo, Hokkaido

COMPLETED 2013

FLOOR AREA 950 ft²

SITE AREA 860 ft²

This three-story timber-frame house occupies a long, narrow lot. In order to preserve the clients' privacy and to take advantage of the difficult site, the architect sought to create frequent connections between interior and exterior space and to multiply the number of small volumes within the house. There are in fact no less than 32 "rooms" or sub-spaces within the house, organized around a central spiral stairway. The exterior of the house is clad in galvanized, corrugated metal plates, insuring its durability. The structure is "super-insulated" because of Hokkaido's cold winter climate; the division of the interior into so many small spaces also increases heating efficiency and rapidity. The strategy of subdividing interior space such that it creates a continuum, where outside and inside frequently interact, gives an overall impression of a more generous volume than the external envelope would indicate. This solution—like many of those employed by Japanese architects—depends of course on the clients' willingness to accept quarters that might be considered cramped in the West.

A | Bedroom
B | Wind Buffer Room
C | Closets
D | Study

E | Master Bedroom
F | Living Room
G | Storage

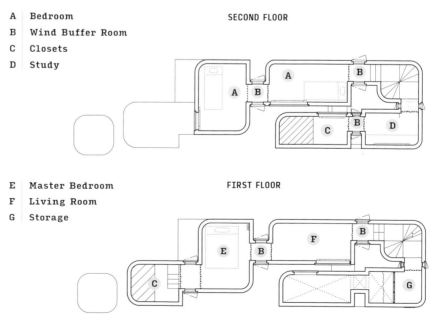

SECOND FLOOR

FIRST FLOOR

Taking advantage of the Japanese adaptatibility to small spaces, the architect divides this house, where white walls and light wood dominate, into even more volumes than its program might imply.

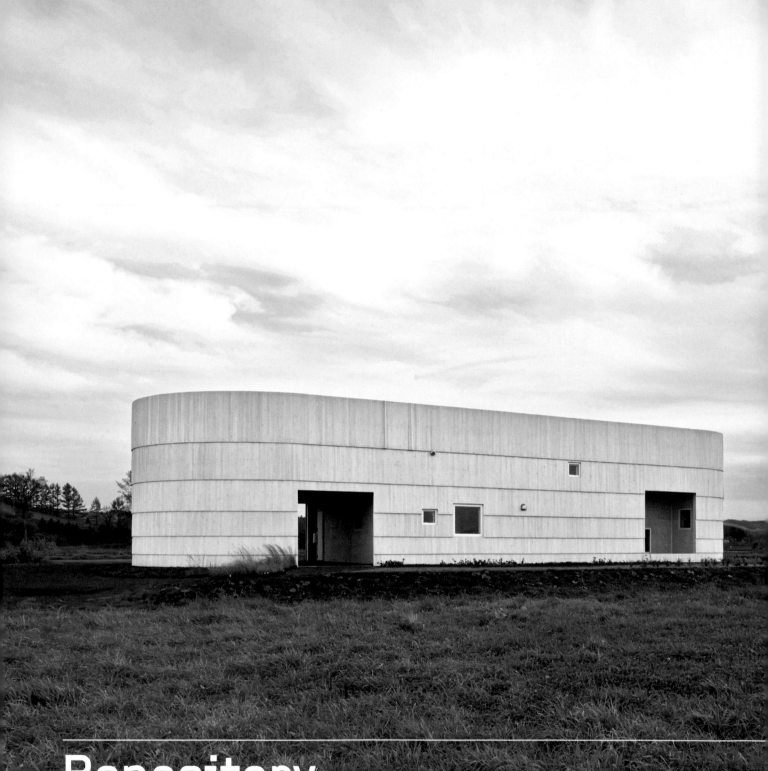

Repository

Jun Igarashi Architects

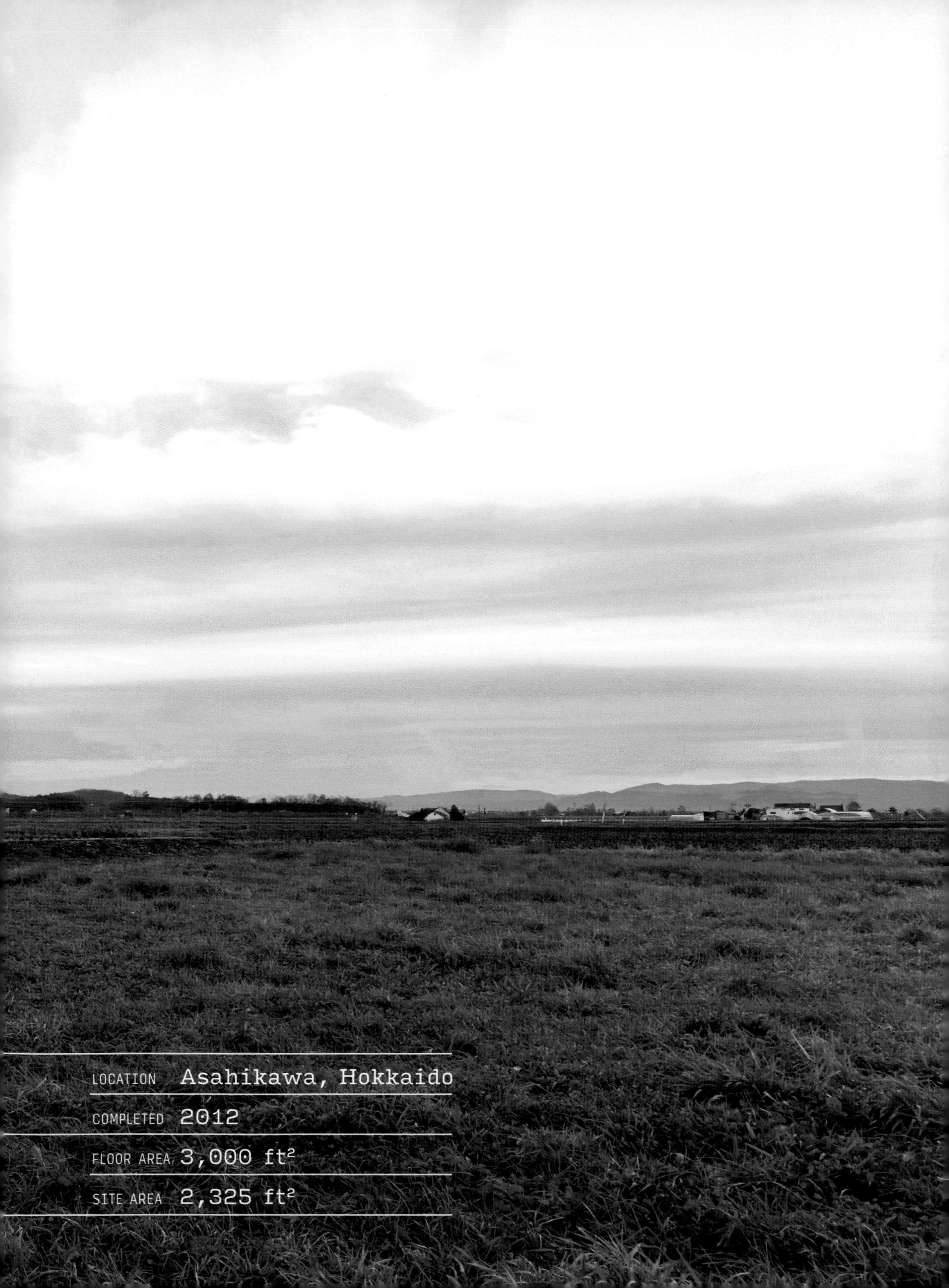

LOCATION   Asahikawa, Hokkaido

COMPLETED   2012

FLOOR AREA 3,000 ft²

SITE AREA   2,325 ft²

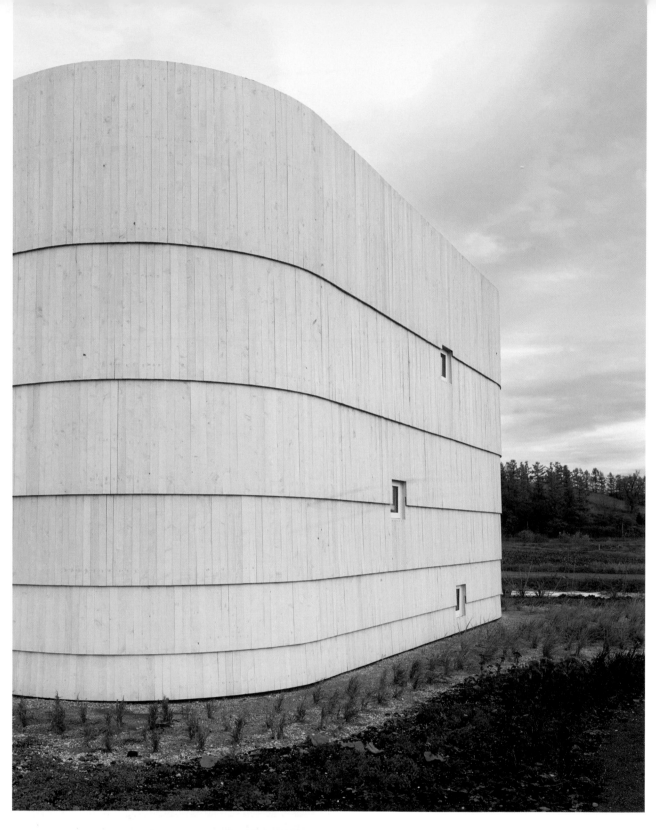

In some respects evocative of a fort or an industrial structure, this house in fact takes its cues from the seasonal cold and snow. The architect deliberately creates a contrast between the wooden forms of the structure and the surrounding green field.

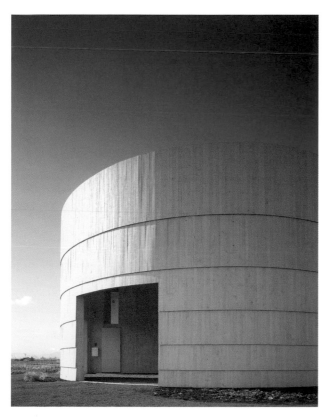

This timber-frame residence, with two levels above grade, is located on a spacious site on the outskirts of Asahikawa, the second largest city of Hokkaido. The site required that the architect consider the relationship of the house with the area and landscape. With temperatures reaching from 90°F in summer to 20° in winter, the house was designed with small openings and is highly insulated. Hokkaido pine is used for the exterior walls because, as Jun Igarashi explains, "of its good thermal conductivity." The living room, dining room, and master bedroom are surrounded by smaller rooms, creating a buffer zone that improves thermal performance and, according to the architect, "can also connect human psychology with the surrounding environment." The rather igloo-like exterior of the house, which sits alone in a green field, gives way to a somewhat warmer interior, in which white walls contrast with wooden beam ceilings, floor, and furniture. The basic plan of the house is rectangular, with a rounded edge to the rear and a rounded parking area in front. The upper-level spaces are reached via a broad spiraling staircase with an almost organic appearance. Skylights and numerous openings give the whole interior a continuous feeling that is highlighted by materials and colors as well as by the presence of suffused natural light.

Jun Igarashi Architects

Jun Igarashi was born in Hokkaido in 1970. He was educated at the Hokkaido Central Kougakuin Technical College (1990) and set up his own practice in 1997.

jun-igarashi.com

A contrast between wood ceilings, floors, and furniture and white walls marks the interior space, as does a spiral staircase that saves space and preserves the harmony of the volumes. Openness between the two levels also characterizes this design.

A	Storage
B	Living Room
C	Washroom
D	Dining Room
E	Windbreak Room

F	Terrace
G	Living/Dining Room
H	Storage
I	Kitchen

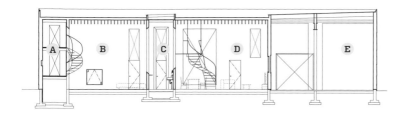

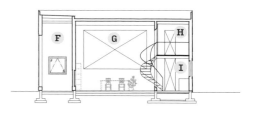

REPOSITORY

House with Plants

junya.ishigami+associates

LOCATION   Tokyo

COMPLETED   2011

FLOOR AREA 745 ft²

SITE AREA   1,240 ft²

The area in which this house was built is characterized by rows of "ready-built" detached houses; by contrast, this steel-frame house stands at a maximum height of 22 feet, though it is just one story. Junya Ishigami states, "I decided to plan a small and beautiful garden amongst this monotonous and artificial streetscape." A light steel frame, clad in Wood Wool Cement Board, surrounds the site, leaving natural soil inside the house's perimeter, where the architect created a terrace surrounded by small plants and trees. An upper terrace also allows the garden to be viewed from above. A kitchen cabinet, bookcase, dining table, and kitchen take their place in this garden, placed as though they were "equivalent elements of a small landscape." A large window opens to the street, giving residents the impression that they are as much outside as the passersby in the street.

For the architect, "In planning this residence, the act of making architecture and creating a landscape held equivalent value. The exterior was to be as man-made as possible, so as to blend in with the landscape of the city. The interior space was to be as close to nature as it could be, in order [for the residents] to be able to lead a rich lifestyle within the city." Like a number of his colleagues of the same generation, Ishigami is clearly seeking ways to break down the barriers that have ruled modern residential architecture for some time. He says, "I had thought about wanting to investigate a new open-mindedness and a new affluence that architecture could have. Beyond that, I feel that one can glimpse the possibility of a new environment created through architecture, as yet unknown to us."

A	Kitchen
B	Garden
C	Lower Terrace
D	Bathroom
E	Upper Terrace

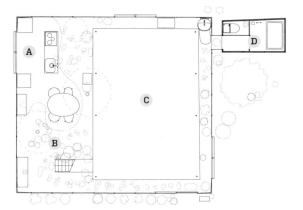

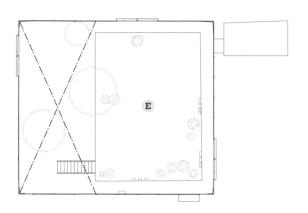

This design is certainly related in its conception to the architect's installation for the Japanese Pavilion at the 2008 Venice Architecture Biennale, where he placed greenhouses with interior vegetal landscapes around an existing building.

junya.ishigami+associates
Junya Ishigami was born in Kanagawa in 1974. He worked in the office of Kazuyo Sejima & Associates from 2000 to 2004, establishing junya.ishigami + associates in 2004. Since then, he has emerged as one of the more significant young Japanese architects.

jnyi.jp

Ellipse Sky
Keiko + Manabu

LOCATION   Tokyo

COMPLETED   2012

FLOOR AREA 7,675 ft²

SITE AREA   4,190 ft²

Ellipse Sky, a four-story apartment building, was the first building completed by Keiko + Manabu. The client invited three architectural firms, each led by a female principal, to participate in a limited competition. Keiko Uchiyama and Manabu Sawase won the competition in part thanks to the 1:20 scale model they presented to the client, which helped explain this formally daring building. The top two floors of the concrete structure are occupied by a 2,960-square-foot duplex apartment for the clients, an obstetrician and his wife. The third floor of this upper duplex has the living and workspace, as well as the kitchen and an outdoor terrace sheltered by the great curve of the facade. The top floor contains two bedrooms and a bath. Because of the building's sloping rear roof, it occupies a smaller floor area than the lower levels. Another area is reserved for the client's mother, and additionally there are four small,

430-square-foot duplex apartments on the bottom two levels that are rented out. The plan of the building is slightly skewed away from a perfect rectangle at the front, due to the lot's shape.

Although the structure initially appears as a concrete box, the architects have completely intervened in the exterior form with a series of large, curving openings in the 9-inch-thick concrete. Smooth urethane-coated concrete surfaces reappear inside the building, notably in the unusual spiral staircase that reaches up from the street-side at ground level to the top floor. Calling on their experience as designers of commercial interiors, the architects were careful to harmonize the unusual openings of Ellipse Sky with the building's interior spaces.

Broad elliptical or semi-circular cut-outs render the facade of this apartment building easily recognizable. They create passageways and terraces, but do not reveal much of the interior design.

Wooden floors and furniture are bathed in natural light that comes from overhead skylights and broad semi-circular windows. A section drawing shows the importance of the spiral staircase that unites the floors of the building.

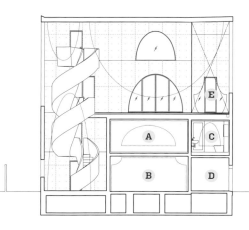

A	Bedroom
B	Garage
C	Bathroom
D	Bike Storage
E	Terrace

Keiko + Manabu

Based in Tokyo and Seattle, the design team of Keiko Uchiyama and Manabu Sawase founded Keiko + Manabu in 2005. Their projects vary from jewelry to product design, commercial architecture, and urban planning for Japanese and international clients.

www.keikomanabu.com

House in Saikai

Daisuke Maeda

LOCATION Saikai, Nagasaki

COMPLETED 2008

FLOOR AREA 1,240 ft²

SITE AREA 13,025 ft²

An illustration of structural
lightness and openness,
this house has a symbolic
tree growing through its roof
from an enclosed courtyard.

Set near a bamboo forest and mountain scenery, this structure has a relatively simple plan: two intersecting squares of different sizes. The architect explains that there are only two elements in his design: the roof and walls. He compares the roof to an inside-out umbrella, and the walls are metaphorically likened to a windmill. Of the design, Daisuke Maeda says, "The windmill begins to turn when the wind blows. Like that, nature flows inside when we walk. The residents feel the atmosphere of nature everywhere: the movement of the sky, the sun, clouds, greenery, and the wind." The architect is clearly interested in maintaining ambiguity in the relationship between interior and exterior. While wood might be expected on the floor, here it is found on the ceiling. Large openings blur the division between interior and exterior, but also, as Maeda says, allow the owners to live in contact with nature in its various forms. A small glass-walled inner courtyard shelters a tree that extends through the flat roof of the structure through a square aperture. Where a Western conception usually seeks to make a clear distinction between the built and the natural, the House in Saikai demonstrates the Japanese expression of nature not only in planted gardens, but also in views and in the presence of the sun and wind.

Inside, the smooth surfaces of the
house almost seem to define
outdoor spaces, transitioning from
courtyard and white walls to an
expanse of sky marked by the broad,
angled, wooden roof.

Daisuke Maeda
Daisuke Maeda was born in 1978 in Nagasaki. He worked from 2004 to 2007 with Suppose Design Office (see page 256). He created his own office, Sequence Studio, in Hiroshima in 2008.
www.sequence-st.com

A   Bedroom
B   Bathroom
C   LDK
D   Central Courtyard
E   Car Port

HOUSE IN SAIKAI   197

Frame
Keisuke Maeda

LOCATION Hiroshima

COMPLETED 2012

FLOOR AREA 1,200 ft²

SITE AREA 1,420 ft²

With the wooden frame that gives this house its name, the architect plays on the division of public and private space, setting the house back from the street, but also creating a small garden with a tree that marks the transition from one realm to another.

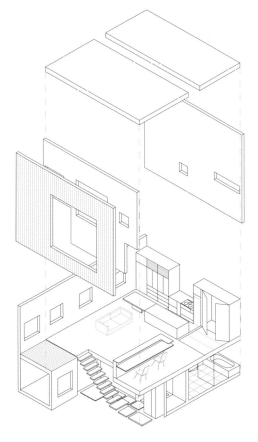

A bedroom, guest room, and bath areas are located on the ground floor of this wood house; the living, dining, and kitchen spaces are on the second floor. "Basically the house is designed like a single integral room measuring 23 by 23 feet," explains the architect, "while attempting to make each space as small as possible." In general, interiors are finished with wood flooring and a plasterboard ceiling. A small garden and a second-floor terrace allow residents to have contact with the outdoors despite the site's limited size. The garden is framed by a large, square opening in the burnished black exterior of the house, from which a tree emerges, growing in the direction of the street. The white inner surfaces contrast with this frame, as does the natural presence of the tree and garden. The stone paving of the exterior garden is also present once inside the sliding door, heightening the impression of a direct connection between interior and exterior. Keisuke Maeda says, "In this house it is possible to live each day feeling gentle breezes, under the natural daylight."

EXPLODED
AXONOMETRIC

+Node
Keisuke Maeda

LOCATION **Fukuyama, Hiroshima**

COMPLETED **2012**

FLOOR AREA **1,345 ft²**

SITE AREA **7,675 ft²**

Located in Fukuyama, the second largest city in Hiroshima Prefecture, this house neighbors a wooded zone to the south and a tiered residential area to the north. The site is notable for the 33-foot difference in height between the property's frontage and its back; for this reason, the architect imagined the house as a node between natural and man-made space. The 1,345-square-foot steel structure has a cladding of cedar panels, interiors finished with cherry wood floors, and walls and ceilings of structural plywood. The architect states, "by placing a 11.5-foot-cube, similar to a wooden bird house, on its side, just like toy building blocks, we created a place that responds to the surrounding horizontal and vertical territory that connects the ground surface to the forest."

This apparently buried cube is part of a larger rectangular lower volume that contains the master bedroom, bath, and a child's room. The lower volume has a rooftop terrace and supports the main, cantilevered block containing a study, living room, kitchen, and dining space. This volume rises to a maximum of 12.8 feet above grade, and houses the kitchen and dining area at its cantilevered end. The cantilevered extremity is 33 feet above the forest floor; it features a large opening through which a tree grows. This opening also frames the view of the forest from inside the house, and emphasizes the idea of the reconciliation between nature and built structure.

The wood-clad house is cantilevered over a wooden hillside. Its projecting volume has a large rectangular opening that seems to reach out and capture nature.

A	Entrance
B	Living Room
C	Bathroom
D	Kitchen/Dining Area
E	Study
F	Terrace

EXPLODED AXONOMETRIC

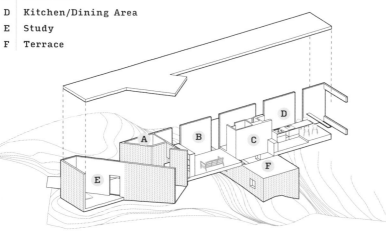

Keisuke Maeda
Keisuke Maeda was born in 1974 in Hiroshima. He established UID Architects there in 2003.

www.maeda-inc.jp

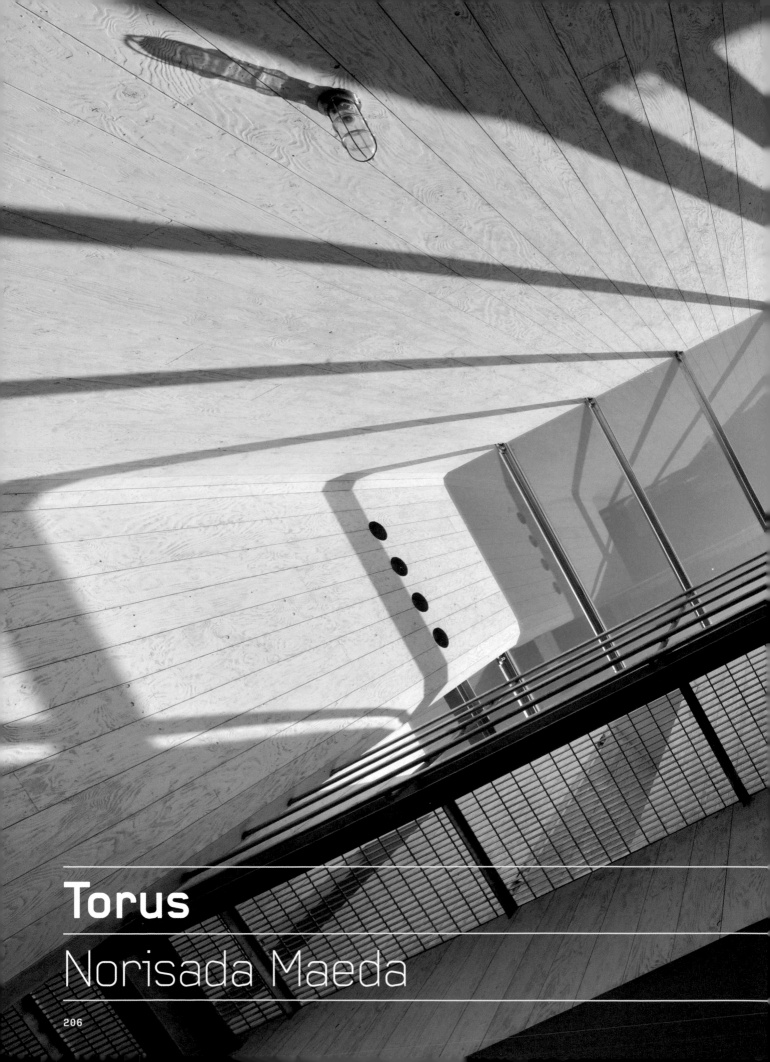

Torus
Norisada Maeda

LOCATION Saitama

COMPLETED 2013

FLOOR AREA 1,560 ft²

SITE AREA 1,820 ft²

While strongly attached to tradition, the Japanese can also prove very audacious clients, particularly for residences. Here, a tranquil inner space is surrounded by typical above-ground telephone and electrical lines.

NORISADA MAEDA

The architect describes this house as a "white, half-amorphous box floating on a lower layer surrounded by glass and perforated aluminum panels." He even compares the appearance of the largely blank upper block to a "heavily armed tank . . . defending the rather indoorsy life of the client's family." The upper unit has an irregular surface texture and color comparable to rough pottery, due to the repeated application, by hand, of a waterproof mortar. This concept has an unusual origin: a photograph of the sky above the building was taken on the day of the completion of the structural frame; the picture was then "abstracted into a gray-scale" image that was reproduced on the building's four sides, carefully applied with thicknesses varying from zero to 1.2 inches. At ground level, the open, glazed corner of the building constitutes the entrance to a pet shop owned by the client, with the two-story residence hovering above it rather ominously. The architect states, "On a cloudy day, the floating mass looks as if it blends in with the sky, its edges losing their individual materiality as they melt into the clouds in the background. Torus is a rare piece of architecture that looks much better under clouds than clear sky."

Inside the building, an atrium contains the kitchen, with catwalk-type bridges leading to the private spaces. Light, vertical plywood planks are used inside, in contrast with the dark floor tiles. The architect states clearly that "cheap" plywood was used, cut into 8-inch-wide boards then treated manually to allow the harder grain to stand out.

Norisada Maeda
Norisada Maeda was born in
Tokyo in 1960. He studied at the
Kyoto University Department of
Architecture, Faculty of Engineering,
graduating in 1985. He founded his
own firm in Tokyo in 1990.

www.maeda-atelier.com

Despite the rectangular plan of the
house, the interiors seem full
of curving surprises and the usual

presence of natural light, brought in
from above but also by ground-level
glazing.

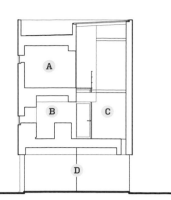

A   Bedroom
B   Tatami
C   Living Room
D   Pet Store
E   Bathroom
F   Terrace
G   Living Room

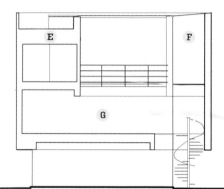

The Rose
Norisada Maeda

LOCATION Tokyo

COMPLETED 2004

FLOOR AREA 3,110 ft²

SITE AREA 1,615 ft²

Located in the Minato Ward of Tokyo, this reinforced concrete structure reaches a maximum height of nearly 33 feet for three floors above grade and a basement. In an unusual description of their work, the architects compare this building to a "rectangular pudding" from which three "lumps" have been scooped out, creating "recto" and "verso" volumes; recto means the air filling three concave openings in the pudding's outer surface, while verso corresponds to the "inside of the scooped-out pudding's volume." The functions with a close relationship to the exterior or public spaces have been placed in the recto area: a parking area, entrance, and lounge. The more private space of the verso contains the bedroom, study, and garden. Visible surfaces both inside and out are in exposed concrete. The basement contains two bedrooms, a guest room, a gym, a storage area, and a garden. The second floor has a bedroom and work space. The top level contains the lounge and a bathroom. The broadly glazed cutouts in the building's facades permit natural light, of course, and glow from within at night. The parking area is inserted into one of these openings at ground level, making it very much a part of the overall design. The steel and concrete interior has a rather industrial appearance that fits well with the concrete used both inside and out.

The architect refers to parts of the
house that have been "scooped
out" to create large openings, as if
sculptured or drilled away from
an originally solid concrete cube.

THE ROSE

Transitional spaces contrast hard materials and a variety of lighting situations, while by contrast the living space in light colors opens itself fully to the urban environment.

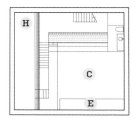

A	Guest Room	F	Entrance
B	Garden	G	Parking
C	Bedrooms	H	Study
D	Gym	I	Bathroom
E	Storage	J	Lounge

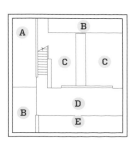

BASEMENT FLOOR

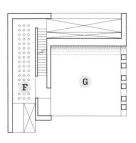

FIRST FLOOR

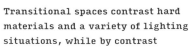

SECOND FLOOR

THIRD FLOOR

House J

Keiko Maita Architect Office

LOCATION Shunan, Yamaguchi

COMPLETED 2012

FLOOR AREA 1,055 ft²

SITE AREA 1,355 ft²

Given that this house is located on a tight site surrounded by other residences, an important consideration was assuring the client's privacy and seclusion. The three-story steel-frame structure with relatively dark wood cladding was designed around a small inner garden. The first floor of the U-shaped structure contains the dining room, kitchen, and family space. The double-height living room and other spaces look out onto an enclosed garden that creates a light well, an important factor given the house's relatively closed exterior. The second floor has a study and reading area, and the bedroom is on the top level, with a roof terrace that looks down into the garden, uniting the three levels. The architect states that the inner garden emphasizes the continuity between interior and exterior but also appears to increase the size of the house.

The house has a relatively closed wooden profile but its interior is brought to life by an inner courtyard with a tree. This private space represents the small, enclosed presence of nature that Japanese people appreciate greatly.

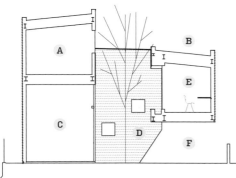

Keiko Maita Architect Office

Keiko Maita was born in 1978 in Yamaguchi Prefecture. She worked with the Shuhei Endo Architecture Institute (see page 102) before creating her own firm in Tokyo in 2008.

www.maitakeiko.com

A	Bedroom	D	Inner Garden
B	Terrace	E	Study
C	Living Room	F	Garage

Shore House
Mount Fuji Architects Studio

LOCATION Manazuru, Kanagawa

COMPLETED 2012

FLOOR AREA 3,210 ft²

SITE AREA 10,740 ft²

The two-story wood-frame Shore House is located on the Manazuru Peninsula, within sight of the Pacific Ocean. The architects devised a series of L-shaped wall and roof units supported by natural wood beams and columns. The principal architect, Masahiro Harada, explains, "These units were prepared in three different scales: large, medium, and small. By positioning them such that each partially overlaps with the others, the varying internal and external heights create terraces and irregular corners in different locations. The positions and angles were not determined conceptually by a strict geometry, but rather scaled in reference to a variety of specific influences, such as the landscape's natural contour lines and sightlines to the sea, the location and canopy of existing trees, the voices of the materials expressed through their volume, texture, and density, and considerations of the balance between fluidity and solidity." In this way, the "personality" of the surrounding environment has been made to enter into a dialogue with the architecture. Made up essentially of two rectangular volumes set at an angle to each other, the flat-roofed weekend house has three bedrooms, a study, a double-height living room, and a workshop on the lower level, with dining and loft areas above as well as a terrace. The rear of the living space is lined by bookshelves, opposite broad expanses of glazing facing the ocean.

This house, unusually ample by Japanese standards, seems to stretch to a neighboring lake through its large wooden terrace and full glazing.

**EXPLODED
AXONOMETRIC**

Mount Fuji Architects Studio
Born in 1973 in Yaidu, Shizuoka
Prefecture, Masahiro Harada worked
in the office of Kengo Kuma and with
Lapeña Torres in Barcelona before
founding Mount Fuji Architects in
2004 with Mao Harada (b. 1976 in
Sagaminara, Kanagawa Prefecture).
www14.plala.or.jp/mfas/fuji.htm

The interior of the house has double-
height shelving on one side and
a view of the landscape on the other.
Volumes interpenetrate each other
freely, aided by such devices as a
cantilevered stairway.

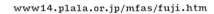
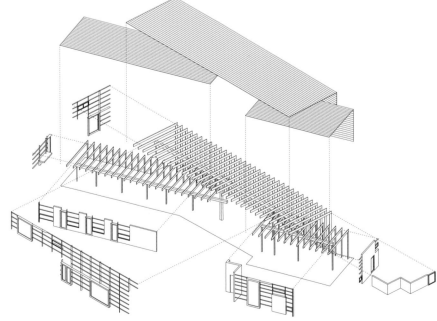

Lighted Valley
Nakae Architects, Inc.

LOCATION **Kanazawa, Ishikawa**

COMPLETED **2014**

FLOOR AREA **1,185 ft²**

SITE AREA **1,785 ft²**

This small wood-frame house was built on a newly developed hillside site. Although the architect, Yuji Nakae, has placed an emphasis on natural light in previous projects, here he judged that large windows would be inappropriate for reasons of privacy, given that the lot is soon to have several neighboring houses. Skylights, found to generate too high a heat load, would be similarly problematic. The architect explains, "Our design solution was to position two rectangular parallelepipeds along the southern and northern borders of the site and to provide light through the gap between them, like a beautiful light shining on a valley." The 16.5-foot-high southern volume contains the double-height living room and kitchen. The other block, containing the rest of the spaces of the house, is 24.5 feet high. The two sections are joined together by a 10-foot-high triangular wood-clad volume. The inner facades of the two main rectangular blocks are fully glazed and reinforced with Vierendeel trusses. They are set at an angle to each other, opening to the rear of the house and admitting daylight. Within the house, the use of wood is privileged, in contrast with the metallic skin of the main volumes. Lighted Valley, concludes the architect, "is an abstract landscape, conceived within a small suburban house, and intended to provide various spatial experiences that one would usually have only in a complex natural landscape."

Nakae Architects, Inc.
Yuji Nakae was born in 1975 in Kanazawa. He worked with Endoh Design House EDH (see pages 106 and 110) until he formed Nakae Architects in Tokyo in 2004.

`nakae-a.jp`

Taking the form of two skewed rectangular volumes of different heights joined by a third triangular space, the house looks relatively blank from the street side but comes to life inside through a carefully considered mixture of materials and lighting conditions.

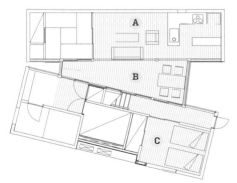

A	LDK
B	Inner Courtyard
C	Bedroom

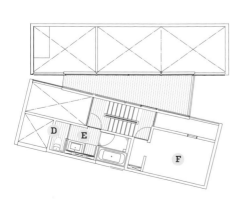

D	Lavatory
E	Bathroom
F	Study

LIGHTED VALLEY

House U

Satoshi Okada Architects

LOCATION **Tokyo**

COMPLETED **2013**

FLOOR AREA **4,845 ft²**

SITE AREA **3,110 ft²**

As seen from the street, the notched
concrete facade is severe, or nearly
blank. Inside, open spaces with
natural light that comes mostly from
above are certainly strict, but create
a carefully ordered, protected space.

House U is located in the prestigious embassy area of
Tokyo. Built on a relatively generous site (about 40 x
78 feet), the spacious structure of reinforced concrete
and steel has three rectangular-plan levels. The
material vocabulary is travertine, granite, wood, and
glass. The architect explains that his client wanted
a house strong enough to resist major earthquakes,
fires, and in particular the somewhat neglected risks
created by "long cycle vibration damage." He responded
by surrounding the building with three-story-high
concrete walls that also serve to block views of the house
from a tall apartment building located across the street.

Local building regulations required a courtyard in
the house. In seeking to interpret this, Satoshi Okada
found inspiration during a visit to Venice and decided to
place a "transparent glass wall" inside the concrete
periphery. The concrete was finished on the upper levels
with light yellow plaster, inside of which residents would

feel as if they were in an "integrated sphere beyond
glass walls." The lower part of the concrete wall
was left bare, giving a sense of scale to the enclosure.

To respect another zoning regulation, the building is
stepped down to the north, which means that each floor is
a bit smaller than the one below. The courtyard includes
a waterfall and pond, and serves as both sculpture
garden and passage to the main upstairs entrance.
A garage and library are adjacent to the courtyard at
ground level, a child's room is above the library, and
the master bathroom is at the top of the structure. The
double-height living area is topped by a concrete roof
slab primarily supported by a large concrete beam. Glass
walls look out onto the courtyard, and the living room
is also lit from above by a skylight. The main bedroom is
suspended above the dining area with a steel structure.
Bedrooms have a transparent glass wall, but their privacy
is protected by a continuous vertical blind.

As the plans show, the house has an enclosed exterior courtyard. Though it is mostly stone, this courtyard brings light and breeze into the house. Interior spaces alternate wood and a broad opening on the courtyard.

A | Garage
B | Bathroom
C | LDK
D | Inner Courtyard

FIRST FLOOR

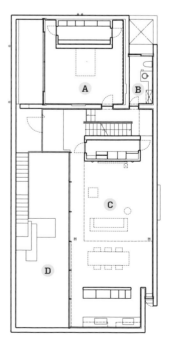

E | Bathroom
F | Children's Room

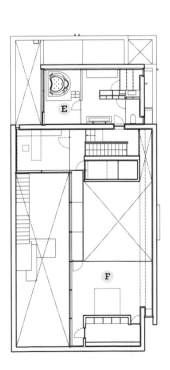

Villa A

Satoshi Okada Architects

LOCATION **Karuizawa, Nagano**

COMPLETED **2012**

FLOOR AREA **4,680 ft²**

SITE AREA **24,940 ft²**

The Villa A, or Villa in Karuizawa, is a steel and reinforced concrete structure that contrasts marble, granite, and lava stone with wood flooring and tatami mats inside. Satoshi Okada states, "In this project, I try to integrate architecture and landscape into designing a whole environment in cooperation with Paul Smither, a British horticulturist active in Japan today." The large triangular site in Karuizawa, one of the most popular summer resorts for Tokyo residents, offers views of a broad natural area and features old trees and bamboo, but is close to another house on the east side. Local regulations required a sloped roof and a 33-foot setback from the road, and dictated that the house could not exceed two stories in height. A semi-underground area

in reinforced concrete houses the bedrooms, a guest room, library, and a bathroom with laundry. The garage and entrance are located below grade and are accessed through a short tunnel. The public areas are above grade, with a living, dining, and kitchen area in a steel part of the structure with glass walls.

The house has an unusual pointed and curved oval plan. The roof is made of 6-inch-thick sandwiched panels of Corten steel with internal lattice ribs. The curved roof is "intended to shelter the upper building with an image of a bird's wing, fully extended, brooding over a nest. It also functions to softly hide the neighboring building on the east."

Extreme simplicity is the rule inside the house, where full-height glazing and sparse furnishings seem to open the space to the natural setting. Seen from below, the red outer shell protectively wraps the interior.

Satoshi Okada Architects

Satoshi Okada studied at Columbia University's Graduate School of Architecture, Planning and Preservation. He founded his office in 1995, specializing in residential architecture, but also commercial and religious commissions, in Japan and Europe.

www.okada-archi.com

The curving form of the house, as seen in the plan, is also sensed within the house, especially in spaces where interior and exterior seem to come together.

EXPLODED
AXONOMETRIC

Tsuchihashi House

Kazuyo Sejima & Associates

LOCATION   Tokyo

COMPLETED   2012

FLOOR AREA 775 ft²

SITE AREA   335²

As is frequently the case in Tokyo, the site of this house is closely surrounded by other residences, but the Tsuchihashi House (or T House) has a full-height atrium that allows light to penetrate into the entire residence. Also thanks to this atrium, the spaces of the house appear as a continuum, much more so than if the architect had opted for closed floor plates. The living area is set partially below grade, with the kitchen and dining space on the ground floor and a bathroom and bedroom one level above. A terrace near the bathroom and a roof balcony allow residents to have contact with the outdoors and the sky. Carefully placed windows bring in more natural light, while preserving the client's privacy.

Thin 1-inch corrugated steel decking on ⅛-inch steel plates form the floors of the house, with open metal stairways linking each level. In fact, the entire aluminum-clad steel supporting structure of the building is exposed inside. Though the use of metal components gives the house a slightly industrial appearance, the white surfaces and the presence of light throughout the residence represent a willful contrast with the dense surrounding urban environment. There is an intellectual and architectural honesty in this configuration—essentially a statement that what you see is what the building really is, an important distinction with many works of contemporary architecture that tend to dissimulate more of their substance.

A | Terrace
B | Study
C | Bedroom
D | Kitchen
E | Dining Room
F | Living Room

The most remarkable element of the design of this house is visible here: the light-filled interior of the residence has a nearly empty core, with mezzanine levels perched throughout.

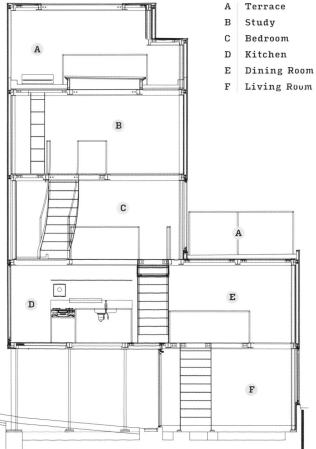

Kazuyo Sejima

Born in 1956, Kazuyo Sejima worked in the office of Toyo Ito before establishing Kazuyo Sejima & Associates in Tokyo in 1987. In 1995, she and Ryue Nishizawa cofounded SANAA, winner of the 2010 Pritzker Prize. Through the design of characteristic white, light-filled buildings that redefine the concept of space, such as the Rolex Learning Center (EPFL, Lausanne, 2009) and the New Museum (New York, 2007), Sejima is at the top of her profession.

www.sanaa.co.jp

House M
Hiroyuki Shinozaki Architects

LOCATION Tochigi

COMPLETED 2012

FLOOR AREA 320 ft²

SITE AREA 1,500 ft²

Built for two women, this single-story wood-frame building is located in the inland Prefecture of Tochigi. The center of the structure is occupied by a square, 20 x 20-foot living and dining area. Arranged in a radial configuration around this central volume, the angular kitchen, bathroom, bedroom, and storage area comprise the rest of the house. The overall floor plan of the house is thus a kind of spiral of boxes that emerge from the irregular living and dining space. The peripheral spaces are more or less open to the living/dining area according to their function—for instance, the kitchen is fully

open—and can be read as delineated volumes from the exterior, their single-slope roofs inclining toward the central volume.

Gaps between the volumes create space for parking, an entrance, and views of the trees located around the house in a gravel garden that also features a small wooden terrace outside the living room. Windows are placed in locations that permit light but protect the owners' privacy. A flat wood-beam roof and ceiling cover the center of the composition.

A	Bedroom	E	Entrance
B	Lavatory	F	LDK
C	Bathroom	G	Tatami
D	Terrace	H	Kitchen

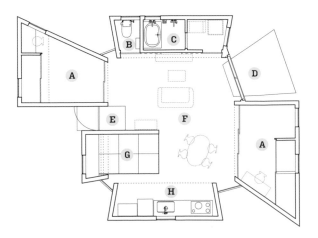

The pinwheel plan of this house
is expressed in its different
slanting or angled volumes. Inside,
a gentle combination of light
wood and white surfaces is coupled
with a variety of windows at
ground level or ringing the upper
level of the living space.

House T
Hiroyuki Shinozaki Architects

LOCATION   Tokyo

COMPLETED   2012

FLOOR AREA 820 ft²

SITE AREA   755 ft²

Intended for a couple, House T is a two-story wood-frame structure located in the center of Tokyo. The exterior walls are covered in resin mortar with fluorocarbon polymer coating; interior walls are of plasterboard. Floors and ceilings are in linden plywood and cement-bonded chipboard (OSB). The architect explains, "We designed the house as a bookshelf. The house has a trapezoidal plan. The floors are bookshelf plates placed at different levels in a deformed box."

Ateliers for the residents are set on the ground floor. The four "bookshelves" on the second floor constitute the living room, and a loft used for reading or storage is located above. Movable furniture, most notably a staircase with integral display cubbies, was custom-made for the house by one of the clients' parents. According to the architect, separating the stairs from the structure enabled him to arrange the different floor levels at irregular heights. "We can give the house complexity and distant views," he says, indicating that the house's open central volume makes each level communicate freely with the others while allowing for an easy reconfiguration of the spaces: the residents can change the rooms' layouts according to their needs. Shinozaki further explains, "The shelf-floors are arranged at each different level in a rigid shelf-frame composed of wooden columns and beams. These floors are fixed partly on the shelf-frame and exterior walls. These details make the floor slabs play a part in the structural system, transmitting vertical and horizontal loads, retaining the idea of a floor that floats freely from its surroundings."

This surprising house is full of holes—the absence of guardrails, which might be mandatory elsewhere, is even more surprising. The space becomes completely flexible—with original features such as a moveable wooden stairway doubling as a storage space.

A | Loft
B | Living Room
C | Dining Room
D | Atelier
E | Entrance

Hiroyuki Shinozaki Architects
Hiroyuki Shinozaki was born in 1978 in Tochigi. He worked in the office of Toyo Ito and created his own firm in Tokyo in 2009, working mostly on private residences.

www.shnzk.com/

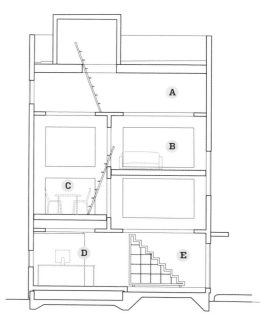

House in Nishiochiai
Suppose Design Office

LOCATION Tokyo

COMPLETED 2013

FLOOR AREA 1,035 ft²

SITE AREA 690 ft²

Completed on a small site not far from Shinjuku, in Tokyo, this house presents itself as a rather austere concrete tower with a trapezoidal plan. Preoccupied, like many of his colleagues, with the difficulties posed by the limitations of residential lots in Tokyo, Makoto Tanijiri of Suppose Design Office sought to propose "a new style of the Japanese small residence in the context of the big city." Stairs that are placed at the periphery of the concrete house's interior extend into the rooms, creating a "fuzzy space without defined borders." A spiral room and large atrium were designed to encourage natural ventilation. Apertures are intentionally sparing in order to create "just enough light." Custom-designed wood furniture is placed on the large landings, which are covered in wood. These landings are broad enough to allow residents to put them to different uses. The concrete underside of the stairway defines the views upward inside the house, giving it a "cozy" feeling, according to the architect, who compares it to a man-made cavern with a few carefully selected openings that permit natural light, including one at the very top of the house.

The austere concrete exterior is echoed in the interior, rendered somewhat warmer by the use of wood floors. Intermediate spaces, usable for various purposes, abound.

Suppose Design Office
Makoto Tanijiri was born in Hiroshima, Japan, in 1974. He created Suppose Design Office in 2000, and has designed over 60 houses since then.

www.suppose.jp

A | Terrace
B | Bedrooms
C | Bathroom
D | Study
E | LDK

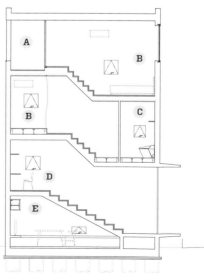

HOUSE IN NISHIOCHIAI   259

Spread Villa

TNA Architects

LOCATION Chino, Nagano

COMPLETED 2011

FLOOR AREA 1,060 ft²

SITE AREA 11,130 ft²

Perched above the forest floor, this ethereal house communicates with the exterior in numerous ways, most obviously through the floor-to-ceiling glazing, and even more directly through a covered outdoor terrace.

A	Bridge
B	Storage
C	Bedroom
D	Play Room
E	Bathroom
F	Courtyard
G	Terrace
H	LDK

Built on a sloped forest site located about three hours from Tokyo, Spread Villa is a steel-frame house with exterior cladding of charred cedar on the lower parts of the walls and cedar and oak flooring inside. The architects explain that the sloped site made them want to "move about like a walking path in the forest," creating a "comfortable relationship between people and nature." Lifted off the ground, the house has a unique relationship with the site that changes as the slope falls away. Approached via a gravel path and a small bridge, the interior of the house is largely open, aside from a few walls placed at unexpected angles. The plan of the house itself forms a square nearly 36 feet on each side, within which the forest itself continues to grow in an open 14.5-foot central courtyard that can be accessed by a canopied door and short stair. Thin-framed full-height glazing almost gives the impression that there is no wall separating living space from forest. With glazing on all sides, residents have views not only of the surrounding forest, but also across the interior courtyard and even underneath the volume of the house, where the slope exposes it most. For the architects, "The place where the natural world comes into contact with artifacts is the origin of architecture."

Gate Villa

TNA Architects

LOCATION   Ibaraki

COMPLETED 2013

FLOOR AREA 4,080 ft²

SITE AREA 12,445 ft²

With its orthogonal pattern of
openings and closed volumes,
Gate Villa includes a number of
planted courtyards. Its low,
white mass confidently stands out
from neighboring houses.

A visibly ambitious project, this single-family residence in a nearly rural area three hours from Tokyo is based on a 23-foot square grid. The large site was actually purchased by the client, who has family roots in the region, as four contiguous lots; it was formerly the site of an old castle. The house appears as an assembly of five square modules in one direction and four in the other, some open and some covered by flat white roofs. Trees grow in the open courtyards, in deliberate contrast to the very ordered white checkerboard design. The walls of the house are hung over grid pillars at various heights. The steel- and timber-frame structure is clad in white-painted cedar on the exterior and interior, as well as Bombay black wood inside. The sense of suspension from the structuring grid frame is achieved inside as well, where living spaces seem to hover just above the earth. Given the very ordered nature of Japanese agriculture, the entire house might be seen as a metaphorical field, carefully planted with different varieties and essences, some natural, others entirely man-made. Parking for two cars, a guest room, and the entrance are set on the southern side of the house, as is the front garden. South, east, and west gardens are located further in as the visitor moves in a northerly direction. The next row of grid space is occupied by a bedroom, living, dining, and kitchen areas. Finally, the north garden, court garden, and vegetable garden neighbor another bedroom and a separate bathroom.

A | Bedroom
B | Study
C | Living Room

D | Dining/Kitchen Area
E | Bathroom
F | Garage

The astonishingly light and open forms of the house blend in almost seamlessly with the enclosed courtyards, assuring ample daylight and contact with nature while preserving privacy.

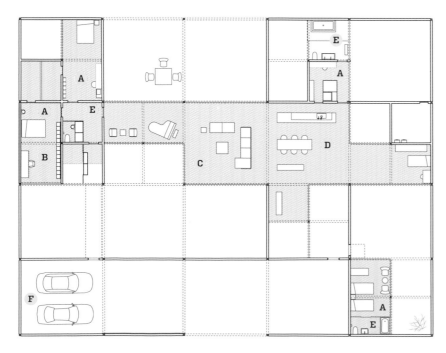

TNA Architects

Makoto Takei (b. 1974) worked
with Atelier Bow-Wow (see pages
46 and 50) and Tezuka Architects
before establishing TNA with Chie
Nabeshima (b. 1975) in 2004.

www.tna-arch.com

Tunnel House
Makiko Tsukada Architects

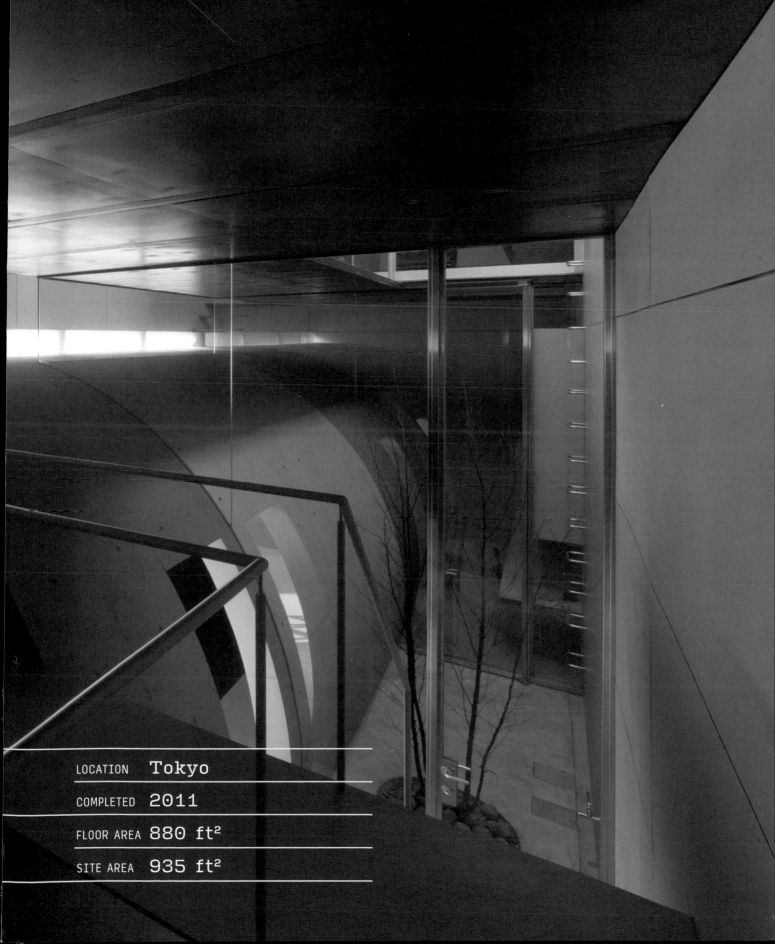

LOCATION **Tokyo**

COMPLETED **2011**

FLOOR AREA **880 ft²**

SITE AREA **935 ft²**

Built with reinforced concrete and steel, this house and office is located in the Suginami Ward of Tokyo. The architect imagined the rectangular plan structure as a "visual extension of the street on the site, creating a virtual crossroads." The interior and exterior spaces are connected by carving out a part of the volume along the extended axis of the street. The carved-out space forms a kind of tunnel or tube that penetrates the interior of the structure. In further explaining this gesture, Tsukada calls on an important concept of Japanese culture, *uchi-soto*, or the distinction between in-groups (*uchi*, inside) and out-groups (*soto*, outside), applied here to spaces. The architect interprets *uchi* as being "in the tunnel" and *soto* as being "out of the tunnel." In the case of this house, two small boxes containing a bedroom and a bathroom form the "tunnel-*uchi*." In the interior space of the "tunnel-*soto*," "the light that cascades down along the tunnel surface from the oblong top light and the light coming down from the courtyard intersect each other three-dimensionally."

Inside, a floating steel floor and an extremely thin (¼-inch) table "give the space a surreal atmosphere of floating and expansion, while creating a sharp contrast with the immense volume of the tunnel." The net result of the architect's exploration of the tunnel concept is that visitors feel that they are outside the house when they are actually inside. "By experiencing repeated reversals of the interior and the exterior spaces (betrayed feelings), one probably can feel a sense of expansion and openness in this tunnel house," says Tsukada.

These interiors are in many ways
typical of contemporary Japanese
residential architecture: light is
present, often brought in from
above; despite a kind of inherent
industrial effect, this interior
evokes a protected space that could be
likened to a kind of urban womb.

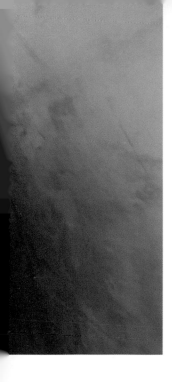

A | Terrace
B | Courtyard
C | Dining/Kitchen Area
D | Car Port

Makiko Tsukada Architects
Makiko Tsukada was born in 1961
in Hokkaido. She worked with
the architect Minoru Takeyama
(1989–93) and with Shigeru Ban
Architects in Tokyo (1993–94) (see
pages 66 and 72) before creating
her own firm, Makiko Tsukada
Architects, in 1995.
makikotsukada-architects.com

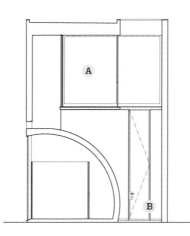

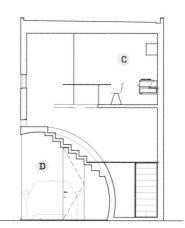

InBetween House

Koji Tsutsui & Associates

LOCATION Karuizawa, Nagano

COMPLETED 2010

FLOOR AREA 1,915 ft²

SITE AREA 21,055 ft²

A wood-frame house with a concrete foundation, the InBetween House was built on a sloped site surrounded by Japanese larch trees. Responding to the client's desire to blend into the natural surroundings and local culture, the architect designed this house in the spirit of a cluster of mountain cottages. The five single-pitched roof cottages were built with traditional Japanese wood construction methods and are clad in larch siding. Gaps between the cottages, set at angles calculated in 30 degree increments, function "like alleys in a city"; this is the "in-between" space referred to in the residence's name. The architect explains, "The design intent of this house is not the final architectural form, but rather, establishing a set of design rules of cottage placements and connections. These allow the house to be freely arranged to satisfy any requirements and adapt to any future changes or additions, prolonging its building life." A new type of radiant heat panel was installed below the concrete floor slabs to save energy use. Operable windows are at each end of the "in-between" spaces to encourage natural ventilation.

Though it seems like a unified whole, the InBetween House is made up of five "cottages," each designed with carefully elaborated interstitial spaces.

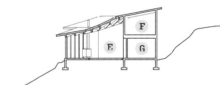

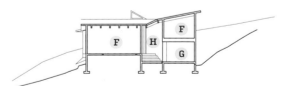

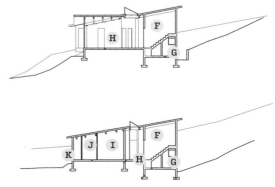

Wooden construction, made with
traditional methods, gives a
warm, chalet-like atmosphere to
the interiors, while details of the
forms evoke a very contemporary
sensibility.

A	Garage
B	Patio
C	Kitchen
D	Dining Room
E	Living Room
F	Lounge
G	Bedroom
H	Sunhall
I	Bathroom
J	Sauna
K	Storage

Bent House

Koji Tsutsui & Associates

LOCATION **Tokyo**

COMPLETED **2012**

FLOOR AREA **800 ft²**

SITE AREA **935 ft²**

KOJI TSUTSUI & ASSOCIATES

This residence's exterior is characterized by powerful angled concrete forms, while interiors mix hard surfaces and generous, shielded openings that let in light and views of outdoor foliage.

Made up of what the architect calls "a collection of three bent boxes," this house is located in the Ota Ward of Tokyo and was built on a site surrounded by other residences. The boxes, each of which has a skylight, form an assembly of entry, study, and main living space. According to Koji Tsutsui, the smaller boxes "stretch out beyond the overhang of the larger box to harvest sunlight," while providing rain protection for the entrance. They also serve as guardrails for the second-floor terrace and bring precious daylight to the first floor, which hardly gets any sun due to the proximity of neighboring houses. The second floor, where the dining area is located, has no divisions, creating an impression of generous space despite the small size of the house. Indeed, in spite of extremely restricted space, the residents enjoy a light-filled house with such features as a sheltered exterior balcony on the upper floor. The architect states, "The bent boxes are in harmony with the sloped rooflines of surrounding houses that are regulated by the building code's height limit. Our design engages light and spaces on the limited site to create a unique experience within the city."

A | Bathroom
B | Bedroom
C | Study
D | Entrance

E | LDK
F | Terrace

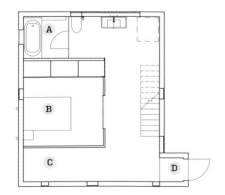

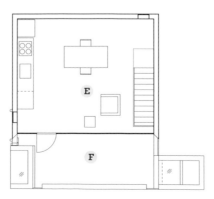

Wood is employed for the stairs,
in thick wooden blocks that project
directly from the concrete wall
with no handrail, confirming the
architect's preference for strong
forms and hard materials.

Koji Tsutsui & Associates
Born in Tokyo in 1972, Koji Tsutsui
worked in the office of Tadao Ando
(see page 30) for several years.
In 2004, he founded his own firm,
Koji Tsutsui Architect & Associates
in Tokyo, adding an office in San
Francisco in 2010.

www.kt-aa.com

Philip Jodidio studied art history and economics at Harvard
before becoming Editor in Chief of the leading French art monthly
Connaissance des Arts (1980–2002). He is the author of more than
100 books on contemporary architecture, including monographs on
the Japanese architects Tadao Ando and Shigeru Ban.

Photo Credits